Matthew James Higgins, William Stirling Maxwell

Essays on social subjects

Matthew James Higgins, William Stirling Maxwell

Essays on social subjects

ISBN/EAN: 9783741172168

Manufactured in Europe, USA, Canada, Australia, Japa

Cover: Foto ©Andreas Hilbeck / pixelio.de

Manufactured and distributed by brebook publishing software (www.brebook.com)

Matthew James Higgins, William Stirling Maxwell

Essays on social subjects

ESSAYS
ON SOCIAL SUBJECTS

BY

MATTHEW JAMES HIGGINS

WITH A MEMOIR

BY

SIR WILLIAM STIRLING MAXWELL, BART.

With Two Portraits

LONDON
SMITH, ELDER, & CO., 15 WATERLOO PLACE
1875

[All rights reserved]

TABLE OF CONTENTS.

	PAGE
MEMOIR OF MATTHEW JAMES HIGGINS .	ix
LIST OF HIS PUBLISHED AND PRIVATELY PRINTED WRITINGS ISSUED IN A SEPARATE FORM DURING HIS LIFE .	lxxi

ESSAYS.

JACOB OMNIUM THE MERCHANT PRINCE. *New Monthly Magazine, August* 1845 .	1
MR. Z., THE HORSE-DEALER. *April* 1843	37
Z. FARM. *April* 1843	47
THE WILD SPORTS OF MIDDLESEX	60
THE FATHER OF THE FANCY .	74
ANIMAL MAGNETISM .	83
THE MAN WHO LIVES FOR HIMSELF. *New Monthly Magazine, September* 1845	95
HORSE-BUYERS AND HORSE-SELLERS .	101

Table of Contents.

	PAGE
*Cornet Rag and Captain Famish	116
*Captain Jack	122
*Sporting Tigers	132
*The Breakdown, a Scene under my Windows in Whitehall, 1836.	145
*The Courier .	152
*Monaco. *Cornhill Magazine*, August 1864	163
*A Day with the Emperor's Hounds. *Cornhill Magazine*, April 1864	194
Reform Your Waltzing. 1845	214
*Our Chapel of Ease. 1847 .	223
*Chelsea Hospital	241

PORTRAITS OF MATTHEW JAMES HIGGINS.

Bust; from a Photograph taken by Kilburn, 1859, *facing title-page*

Full-length; from a Picture by Sir Francis Grant, Pr. R.A.; the Terrier added by Sir Edwin Landseer, 1861, *facing* p. ix

---

* Not included by the author in his privately printed *Social Sketches*, London, 1856; and, with the exception of the two *Essays* from the *Cornhill Magazine*, printed from his MSS., and probably for the first time.

MEMOIR

OF

MATTHEW JAMES HIGGINS.

CONTENTS OF THE MEMOIR.

		PAGE
I.	*Early Life—Trip to West Indies*, 1838	ix
II.	*First Literary Works*, 1835–1846	xxii
III.	*Second Trip to the West Indies*, 1846–7	xxv
IV.	*The Irish Famine*, 1847	xxxiii
V.	'*Morning Chronicle*'	1
VI.	'*The Times*' *and* '*Pall Mall Gazette*'—*Death*	liv
VII.	*Characteristics*	lxiv
	List of the Writings of M. J. Higgins, issued in a separate form during his life	lxxi

MEMOIR.

I.

MATTHEW JAMES HIGGINS was born on December 4, 1810, at Benown Castle, in the county of Meath. He was the youngest child and only son of Matthew Higgins and Janette, daughter of James Baillie of Ealing Grove, second son of Hugh Baillie of Dochfour. His father dying early, he was brought up under the care of his mother. Educated at a private school near Bath, and afterwards at Eton, he went thence to New College, Oxford, where hunting seems to have occupied more of his time and thought than study.[1] In the subsequent

[1] In the National Gallery there is a very fine picture by Gainsborough of James Baillie, his wife and four children. It was bequeathed by Mr. Alexander Baillie, his son, to his nephew Mr. Higgins for his life, and afterwards to the National Gallery. The mother of Mr. Higgins is the eldest girl with the hat and feathers, standing on the right side of her mother. In features as well as in stature, Mr. Higgins bore some resemblance to his grandfather.

years he travelled in Italy and Spain, and frequently passed his winters at Naples, where his three sisters were married to Italians.[1] When in England, London or the house of his mother at Hampstead were usually his head-quarters. It was during one of these winters in Italy, that of 1839-40, that the writer of this notice had the pleasure of making at Rome the acquaintance of the 'gentle giant,' as Mr. Higgins used to be called amongst his friends on account of his stature, which reached the extraordinary height of 6 feet 8 inches. A gentleman of the same name, whose height was about 6 feet 4 inches, used to complain that the overshadowing presence of his namesake caused him to be distinguished amongst his countrymen at Rome as 'little Higgins.'

In 1838 Mr. Higgins went to British Guiana, chiefly for the purpose of visiting an estate which he had inherited in that colony, and the condition of which was not satisfactory. He sailed from Gravesend on September 27, in the 'Louisa Baillie,' a sailing vessel bound for

---

The picture is 8 feet 2 inches in length by 7 feet 5 inches wide.—Wornum's *Catalogue of the Pictures in the National Gallery, British School*, 1875, p. 51, No. 789.

[1] Alicia was Marchesa di Bagnano; Harriet, Baronessa Cicarelli, afterwards Marchesa Casavolpe; and Amelia, Signora Pandola.

Demerara, and landed at Falmouth early in April 1839. Of the outward voyage, his residence in the colony, and the voyage home, he kept a very full and pleasant journal, which evinces the keen observation and graphic power which distinguish his published writings. It also shows that he read a good deal, especially at sea; the pages facing the daily record of events being frequently filled with quotations from the Latin and English authors who were his companions.

In 1838 our West Indian colonies were going through the painful transition stage which followed the emancipation of the negroes. It was a bad time for absentee proprietors, as West Indian proprietors frequently were. The natural indolence of the negro and the fewness of his wants led him to consider the right to do nothing as the first privilege of the freeman. He contracted to perform certain labour, but there was no efficient law to compel him to fulfil his share of the bargain, and the competition of imported industry was yet in the bud. On most estates it was found that production dwindled and expenses of all kinds increased in a manner that was highly alarming. Attorneys and managers, accustomed to the old high-handed rule and easy-going extravagance of the golden age, were slow to discover or adopt the policy and the economy required by the iron age, which had come upon the colonies with no silver or brazen gradation. Mr. Higgins's timely visit probably saved his estate of Affiance from the ruin which overtook many neighbouring plantations. On his arrival there he found awaiting him a petition from his black labourers complaining of unfair treatment in regard of work, wages, and supplies, and especially of the systematic use of their provision grounds as pastures for the manager's cows; and threatening, if these wrongs were not redressed, to seek service elsewhere—a threat which Mr. Higgins discovered they were very loath to put into execution, because of 'the indignity of being forced to become "new niggers" on another estate.' A very cursory examination of affairs on the spot convinced him that both he and his people had long been treated with impartial injustice by his plausible attorney and his gentleman-like manager, who were neglecting his interests, actively making away with his substance, and swiftly destroying what remained of discipline among the blacks. He dismissed both, and supplied their places with men of high character, whom his connections—the Baillies, who had large possessions in the colony—enabled him to obtain. The attorney of his choice was 'a tall, hard-bitten Scotchman, who had taken a prominent part in the affairs of the colony, and one of the most successful of his class.' The manager, also a Scotchman, was a young man of pleasing manners and quick intelligence, for whom Mr. Higgins soon conceived a strong liking. When he had, as he thought, settled everything on a new and safe footing, and was proposing with much satisfaction to make his escape from the prevalent yellow fever, he was compelled to remain another month in Guiana, because the new manager had become jealous of the new attorney, and, in hopes of unseating that functionary, gave up his post at the last moment. Mr. Higgins disappointed him by accepting his resignation and providing him with a successor. All these transactions are related in a very agreeable manner, and the record abounds in notes of many interesting facts, social, political, and statistical, and in vivid pictures of West Indian life, scenery, and manners. A few passages are selected as specimens of Mr. Higgins's early style, and as coming fairly within the scope of the writings comprised in the present volume.

The approach to Madeira is thus described:—

October 11, 1838.—About 10 A.M. we rounded the point and caught sight of Funchal. I cannot say it struck me as being so beautiful as Coleridge and others have represented it to be; but then I have seen Naples, and Genoa, and Cadiz, and Porto Ferrajo to boot, which in its small way is as lovely as any of the before-mentioned beauty-spots of the earth. We were going six knots in smooth water; and, expecting to land in an hour or two, we took ourselves to our cabins to get out our shore-going costume, and shave, and make ourselves once more into gentlemen, when lo! the breeze failed us, and here we are bobbing up and down with a short swell, the sails flapping listlessly to and fro, just opposite to Funchal and about six miles distant therefrom. Four sailors are endeavouring, or rather pretending to endeavour, to tow the vessel in a boat ahead, but it is hopeless work, and they merely yawn and slowly dip their oars in and out of the water to satisfy the captain. A goose flew overboard, whereupon they cast off the tow-line and pulled after it like devils. After pelting it with a stretcher lashed to a line till it was stunned, to make it heave to, the tall ruffian to whom we gave a dollar for being the first to see the land jumped overboard and secured the runaway. We have been hugging ourselves with the thought of one of Messrs. Gordon's or Keir's or Stoddart's good dinners, but now, at 2 o'clock, we are convinced that we shall feed with Captain Moorsom as usual on muscular ducks, corned beef, curry, and probably the very goose we have just seen murdered. Anchored about a mile from shore at about 4 P.M., when the quarantine boat came off, and the health officer, finding that we had two more hands on board than were mentioned in the ship's manifest, refused to give us *pratique* till to-morrow, at which we are considerably sulky.

Here is a good picture of life at sea :—

October 27, 1838.—Heavy squall last night during the middle watch, and consequently a good deal of sea running in the morning. This day month we sailed from Gravesend. It is amusing to observe the different effects of a month at sea on the different constitutions and characters of the passengers. The good-tempered become irritable, the polite morose, the voracious abstemious. One of our party, who, on leaving England, was very facetious on the subject of the mortality amongst new-comers in Demerara—he himself being a seasoned pipkin—and made many excellent jokes respecting the state of alarm into which we should be plunged on our arrival there, has for the last week completely changed his tone. He declares that he feels very unwell indeed, and is constantly applying to me, whom he has laughed at for the last month, for advice and consolation. He is also consuming a vast quantity of the contents of the captain's medicine chest as a precautionary measure, although he is one of the strongest and healthiest men on board. Even old Mrs. B—— is eschewing her carnivorous propensities; her *protégée*, Miss G——, is laid up with a fit of the gout.

The effect of their advance into the tropics on the ship's company is thus pourtrayed :—

October 31, 1838.—Scorching hot day. (The thermometer two days before had been 85° in the shade on deck.) Calm. Heavy swell from S.E. The vessel pitches bowsprit under, and goes half a knot per hour. The man at the wheel looks sleepy and half baked; and is so. Our two dogs lie panting on deck and refuse water, proving they cannot be cooled by such nasty tepid tipple; ever and anon they languidly arise and stalk sulkily across the deck, and then, suddenly relaxing all their joints, plump despondingly down again, as if they never expected or cared to get up any more. We follow their restless example, transferring ourselves from chair to hencoop and from hencoop to skylight from sheer irritability. The ducks and geese crouch down in their pens and look dry and mangy. The fat steward's shirt adheres to his sweaty ribs; he is choleric, and thumps his *aide-de-camp* boy Harry with unusual acerbity. The old lady lunches voraciously on salt meat and mouldy biscuit, which is a very provoking sight to us bystanders who have no appetites. The common black flies become spiteful, and bite even unto the drawing of blood. Cockroaches abound; butter is oil; the pitch melts in the seams of the ship's deck, and adheres to our feet; the only nigger on board is in uproarious spirits; a creole passenger is also unusually lively; also all the canary birds; as for the monkey, he is positively riotous. A shark cruises about slowly under the counter, ogling a piece of pork on the shark-hook; but his appetite is damped, if a fish's appetite may be said to be damped, by the heat, and he touches it not. The temperature of the cabin is hellish.

November 1.—Such a moonlight night! Moonlight in the tropics is as different from moonlight in our dull climate as clear spring water from bilge water. Sat up until twelve listening to 'Will Watch' and certain other naval ditties sung by Merritt, the mate. Having concluded our concert with 'God save the King,' we danced 'Jim Crow' over McGhee's head, shoved a couple of wet ducks into Cameron's cabin through his scuttle which he had left open, and then retired to bed.

In the 'Louisa Baillie' were some common old kitchen chairs which the voracious old lady was taking out, and which, as they stood on the deck, the passengers occasionally used. One of these crazy seats proved unequal to the weight of Mr. Higgins, and broke down under him. 'Never mind, sir,' said the musical mate, 'the old lady pays nothing for them; they are working their passage, and must chance it.'

A scene upon one of the rivers of Guiana is thus pictured :—

Thursday, January 10, 1839.—The Pomaroon here is as wide as the Thames at Putney, a deep rapid silent stream, of clear brown bush-water, gliding swiftly and noiselessly along. On either side is a lofty hedge of forest trees, springing out of the very waters, innumerable varieties of palms, and over them moras, greenhearts, and silk-cotton trees rearing their heads far above the other giants of the forest; magnolias scenting the whole river, parasites of the most gorgeous hue clinging to the branches of this vegetable wall, form one of the most striking scenes European eye ever witnessed. The profound silence which pervades the scene adds to its interest; not a sound is to be heard save the splash of the paddles, not a bird or insect to be seen save occasionally a carrion crow soaring lazily high overhead, or a couple of macaws screaming as they pursue their rapid journey into the interior. Ever and anon a rude corial manned by Indians glides out from the invisible mouth of some small creek, the red men, with their wild staring countenances and long unkempt hair, looking like bad attempts at imitating the human race. They not unfrequently have their whole families, household utensils, and pets, stowed away in boats with them, and are perhaps going some two or three hundred miles off to purchase some absurd article which they could themselves manufacture in a single day. The Indians about here are Caribrice. Towards evening the animal world of South America, which seems paralyzed by the heat of the sun, resumes its spirits. The woods re-echo with the howlings of beasts, the screaming of birds, and with various unearthly sounds produced by strange insects. The hoarse bullfrog, the razor-grinder, the *campanero* or bell-bird, are prominent performers in this strange concert. Owls and bats flit about in thousands; monkeys and baboons stroll as easily and confidently across the line of the highest trees as if they were on *terra firma*. It is really humiliating for man to watch the swift and dashing progress of a baboon across the forest. He throws himself boldly from tree to tree; a break occurs in the line of march: unhesitatingly he casts himself *à corps perdu* into the bush some fifty feet below; and he is none the worse for it, having managed to break his fall instead of his neck by a judicious application of his nervous tail to some prominent branch. He is desirous of attaining the summit of some tall tree: he swarms rapidly up a bush-rope, thin and tough as whipcord, dangling from its branches, and is perched in its summit out of gun-shot in an instant. There he sits chattering and grinning, and probably entertaining as high an idea of man in a South American forest as a man does of a monkey in a cage at home. As the night falls the scene is lighted up by myriads of bright fire-flies and brighter lantern-flies. Here are no mosquitos to torment one. The climate is delightful; white men are here exempt from those deadly fevers which molest them so grievously on the coast.

The great importance of rum as an element in the prosperity of Guiana is thus exemplified :

'The packet from England brings most interesting intelligence to-day,' said a friend. 'What is it?' said I, expecting that the Queen had died suddenly, or O'Connell been made Lord-lieutenant. 'Why, sir, rum has risen a shilling.'

Of the comical society of Hayti the following glimpse is given :—

March 2, 1839.—Entered the harbour of Cape Henry at midday. As we sailed in the 'Pigeon' packet sailed out, carrying off our mails, and four passengers whom she had obtained under false pretences, saying that we were full, and persuading them to rough it in the 'Pigeon' rather than run the chance of losing their passage by waiting for us. The Jamaica steamer was also in the harbour.

The town is large and massively built, the houses of stone, but nearly half of it is in utter ruin; the streets, having also in bygone days been well paved, now look like the beds of torrents with large blocks scattered here and there. No white people are to be seen, but every variety of colour from cream-colour to ebony. Christophe's reign seems to have been the golden age of this town since it fell into the hands of the negroes.

The negro troops! some with one shoe, some with none; some muskets without locks, others without bayonets; ragged uniforms, the worsted epaulettes hanging down in front: half the soldiers with their heads muffled up in a handkerchief—nigger fashion—and a tall shako stuck over all. They looked exactly like chimney-sweepers on May-day, but were not nearly so neat and clean in their apparel. Then the cavalry! fat old niggers with red trowsers of every variety of shade, shoes, white stockings, long spurs strapped on, green coats out at the elbows and everywhere else, and huge cocked hats, bestriding meagre weakly ponies, only kept on their legs by infernally sharp Spanish bits. The only good part of the military establishment were the drummers; there were plenty of them, and they beat their drums right well and indefatigably, whilst a couple of drum-majors went through a series of wonderfully complicated evolutions with a long loaded cane, chucking it up high in the air and catching it behind their back, &c.

I went with Reece to call on the governor, General Bottex, a yellow negro about sixty, a civil old fellow enough; he received us very graciously surrounded by his black *aides-de-camp*, and questioned us concerning the latest news from Mexico with much interest. General Bottex was just the sort of looking person whom we should employ to raise stock in Demerara; some of his aids would make good field niggers enough, while here they make very indifferent field officers. I had great difficulty in not laughing during the audience. It passed off very well; he speaks only French. He told us that Captain Courtenay, R.N., had gone round to Port-au-Prince to arrange a treaty for opening the ports of Jamaica to the Haytian vessels. We dined at an inn kept by Mdlle. Emma; there was also a billiard table much frequented by the Haytian elegants. The young negroes, being naturally slenderly built, make very good dandies, with frock coats and boots and spurs. A good many lads who in our islands would have been megas, were here swaggering about in uniform, cornets of cavalry.

The negro captains and colonels were *impayable*; not one in three wore a shirt. As we were landing, a black captain of infantry in full fig was about to embark from the quay in a small boat; being somewhat the worse for liquor, he tumbled into the water. John Thomas, the coxswain of the cutter, stretched forth his brawny arm, seized the gentleman in gold epaulettes by the collar, and tossed him into his boat head foremost, giving him a most sonorous slap on the breech, '*pour le rassurer*,' as he stumbled over the thwarts. Everybody was extremely civil to us. Indeed, the negroes here have not the forward and assuming manners of our free blacks.

I had great fun with some negro and coloured women, to whom I told that I was the ship's doctor. All the young ladies forthwith insisted on consulting me, and I had to listen to their chattering and prescribe for them until the boat came to take me on board. A great many of them are very pretty. The Haytian money is the vilest dross that ever passed current, and the oddest thing is that the people will not take good Spanish dollars.

Sunday, March 3.—Went ashore at five with the steward, to market. Things were very cheap, but not very good : no oranges except bitter ones ; pineapples twopence a piece ; good beef twopence a pound. The girl who supplied us with poultry was the prettiest negress I have seen, and had teeth whiter than any pearls, kept so, as she informed me, by using a chaw-stick three times a day. The general was riding round to visit the different posts with a train of aids. I defy anybody to caricature them. No sugar is made here. A little coffee and cotton is exported. The packet weighed at six, and got out of harbour with the land wind. When we had finished our marketing we had to pull out six miles to her—rather a hot job.

II.

Although Mr. Higgins's West Indian journal affords good evidence of his love of literature and his skill in the use of the pen, he is not known to have published anything until he had attained his thirty-fifth year.

In 1845 he contributed to the August number (No. 296) of the 'New Monthly Magazine,' then conducted by Mr. Harrison Ainsworth, the paper which stands first amongst the following 'Essays on Social Subjects.' It attracted so much attention that his contribution to the next month's number, 'The Man whom Most of Us Know,' here reprinted under the title which he afterwards gave it of 'The Man who Lives for Himself,' was announced as 'By the Author of Jacob Omnium;' and the name ever afterwards stuck to him through life, and was, indeed, frequently used by him, either at full length or in its initials J. O., as the signature of his letters to the press. It was as a contributor to the 'New Monthly' that he made the acquaintance of Thackeray, who had already written much, but was still little known to the public. Each had been struck by something written by the other; and they applied, almost at the same time, to the publisher to bring them together. The introduction soon ripened into an intimate friendship which was closed only by the death of the great novelist Thackeray has immortalised his friend and his friend's pen-name in the ballad of 'Jacob Omnium's Hoss,' perhaps one of the happiest examples of his rhyming prose. A horse belonging to Mr. Higgins having been stolen from Tattersall's by means of a forged letter, was some weeks afterwards recognised and recovered by his groom in the streets of London. The thief, or the receiver of stolen goods, who had been keeping the horse at livery, finding it convenient to disappear, the stable-keeper brought an action against Mr. Higgins for the animal's keep. The cause was tried in a small and ancient local court called the Palace Court, an institution which had outlived its usefulness, and of which the later proceedings will be chronicled amongst the curiosities of the first decade of the reign of Queen Victoria. Judgment having been given for the plaintiff, the defendant straightway stated his case in so clear a manner in the 'Times,' that the Palace Court in a few months was shut up. The story told in Thackeray's 'Bow Street Ballad' by Policeman X[1] in his own inimitable vernacular, is a very accurate account of the transaction in which Jacob Omnium and his horse played so important a part, and which brought upon the ancient Palace Court the doom of the Star Chamber.[2] When Thackeray had occasion to buy a horse, he usually availed himself of the skill and judgment of his friend. Amongst the many amusing notes and sketches by the great novelist

---

[1] It appeared in *Punch*, 1848, vol. xv. p. 251, under the title of 'Bow Street Ballads,' No. II. 'Jacob Omnium's Hoss,' and is reprinted in Thackeray's Works, 1869, *Ballads and Tales*, p. 211. For sketches of the Palace Court see *Punch*, 1849, vol. xvi. pp. 31, 54.

[2] It was closed on December 31, 1849.

which enriched the scrap-book of Mr. Higgins, we remember one in which an advertisement of a horse for sale cut from the day's morning paper headed the sheet, and the MS. consisted of this couplet:

> 'I read in the "Times" of this wonderful bay cob,
> Now pray, if you love me, go see him, dear Jacob!
> W. M. T.'

'Jacob Omnium's Hoss,' and the dedication to 'The Adventures of Philip'—'In grateful remembrance of old friendship and kindness: Kensington, July 1862,'—commemorate many years' pleasant intercourse and congenial companionship.

III.

In the autumn of 1846, Mr. Higgins determined to take another trip to the West Indies. At the end of October he paid Lord and Lady Ashburton a visit at the Grange, where his journal records that he met Rogers and Carlyle :—

The latter talked much and well, but was very sarcastic, upsetting all Rogers's old-world subjects of reverence most pitilessly. When the ladies returned, Rogers drew his chair up to the fire for a chat, and indulged us with some anecdotes verging on twaddle. Carlyle silently lighted his candle and stole off to bed. As soon as he was gone, Rogers said bitterly, 'That fellow can't bear to hear anyone talk but himself.

On November 1 Mr. Higgins proceeded to Southampton, and next day embarked on the mail steamer 'Medway,' being one of 137 passengers. The accommodation, living, and attendance were all very bad, and the overcrowded vessel was so over-loaded, that until the voyage had consumed a good deal of her water and coal her progress was very slow. To these discomforts was added, during the first week, very rough weather; but it afterwards improved, 'the smutty sails' were set to a fair wind, and 'the engine, which at starting made but seven revolutions in a minute, began to make twelve.'

Here is a sketch of one of the passengers :—

Amongst the various passengers with whom I conversed was a respectable elderly woman, who followed rather a singular calling. She had, she said, a good connection at Bombay, Madras and Calcutta, and twice or thrice every year she conveyed children to and from India. Higher wages, I suppose, had tempted her to deviate from her regular line, and she was now employed in escorting a baby of a few months old to Mexico. It was really admirable to watch the good-humour, dexterity, and patience of the old merwoman, and to witness the superiority which long use had given her over the other females in the ship.

She sought no aid from the cabin servants, was never

sick, had capital sea-legs, and did everything for herself. She knew exactly by the state of the cook's temper when she could, and when she could not, get a supply of hot water from the galley, or warm the child's victuals there, and used to keep her own cabin and her charge's clothes as neat and clean as could be.

She had made friends with one or two of the oldest and hairiest of the seamen, who evidently respected her for her sea-womanship, and often got them to give her a spell at dandling the baby, when she wanted to have a wash or get her meals.

Her chief anxiety appeared to be as to the probability of her procuring in Mexico a return baby or two for Europe.

The old boatswain, a great friend of hers, used irreverently to advise her to try for some black ones, which would not require so much washing; but as he was a kind-hearted fellow, and obviously well skilled in the art of nursing an infant, she did not take offence at his jokes.

On November 11, Madeira was reached and left behind; on the 14th, the 'Medway' was running before the trade-winds with all sail set and her awning spread; and on the 17th she crossed the line,

when Neptune and Amphitrite, represented by the boatswain and carpenter, made a triumphal procession round the ship, and about twenty poor devils were tarred and shaved with a piece of iron hoop, and then tossed into a sail placed in the water, in which they were soundly ducked by Neptune's two horses, a couple of stout sailors clad in sheepskins and cows' tails. Ultimately all the passengers, who had crowded forward to look on, were plentifully watered with warm water pumped from the engine through a hose.

On November 23 the 'Medway' anchored at Barbadoes, and Mr. Higgins passed that afternoon and the next morning in surveying the neighbourhood of Bridgetown. On the afternoon of the 24th he and twenty of his fellow-passengers dined together in the principal inn, 'and took leave of each other most likely for ever.' He afterwards embarked in the 'Reindeer' packet, 'a small, wet, miserable craft, full of rats and cockroaches,' and steamed off for Demerara, where he arrived at noon of the 27th. Next day he again shipped himself in the 'Sugar Plum' at 8, and at 3 P.M. stuck in the mud off Affiance, his own estate, which he found in great prosperity.

Affiance looks well: house improved, buildings in good repair, canes clean and healthy; no crowd of negroes to assail me with complaints, merely a few of the old head people to pay their respects. People working well, and we have no lack of labour. Cultivation in capital order.

On December 5, at 5 P.M., he again sailed for Bridgetown in the 'Reindeer,' crowded and dirty as usual, the confusion being increased by a lady's being brought to bed in the ladies' cabin, which already contained four ladies and six children. Three pleasant days having been spent in the beautiful island of Grenada, Mr. Higgins again joined the 'Medway,' and on the forenoon of the 11th he was in the harbour of Port of Spain, in Trinidad. There he and his friend Sir Robert Brownrigg were invited to become the guests of the Governor, Lord Harris, at his country house of St. Ann's. Their trips to the islands of the Bocas and the Pitch Lake are thus recorded in the journal:—

Friday, December 17, 1846.—Drove down in Lord Harris's omnibus at 7 A.M. to the quay, and embarked with a large party on board the colonial steamer for the islands of the Bocas. Beautiful isles they are, covered with stately timber and rare flowers, and abounding in romantic coves and bays and caverns. They have several pretty settlements of fishermen on them, chiefly Frenchmen, who catch whales during one part of the year and supply the town with fish for the table, the Gulf of Pavia being highly fishful. We breakfasted on board, and dined at a charming little island belonging to a Dr. Nelson, who entertained us most hospitably; saw oysters growing on trees, and ate them stewed moreover. At Monos, picked up Mr. White, the colonial secretary, who had been invigorating his health by cruising on one of these islands for three weeks. He is a *bon vivant*, and arrived on board escorted by a turtle, a large supply of oysters, and three huge sea crawfish. Altogether, it was a most delightful day's pleasuring, though it rained heavily for three hours, and though we hauled the seine and took nothing.

Saturday, Dec. 18, 1846.—Up again at 6, and off in the

same steamer to La Braye to see the Pitch Lake. The steamer was very slow and most heavily laden. We got rid of our passengers at S. Fernando, a very pretty village (as seen from the sea), built at the base of two hillocks. We have picked up Mr. Hume, Mr. Burnley's nephew, who had been visiting estates in the Naparime district, and was going down to La Braye. We gave him some breakfast, which he reciprocated by furnishing us with mules when we arrived at La Braye, showing us his very pretty estate of Mon Plaisir, and giving us a dinner. The Pitch Lake is a most curious sight; it covers many acres—I can hardly guess how many; is traversed by fissures five and six feet deep and as many wide, full of water. In some places, grass and low bushes spring out of it; its surface is hard enough for man and beast to traverse in most places, provided they do not turn, but, on stopping, the feet gradually begin to sink in the warm tough pitch till prudence and regard for one's boots or shoes compel one to move on. The whole lake appears to be in a state of torpid ebullition, slowly yielding up charred stumps and masses of earth from the bottom, wherever that may be. It is 120 feet above the level of the sea. A stream of tough hard pitch imperceptibly tending downward makes its way into the sea at La Braye, and is used as a road to the lake. We returned to La Braye in a cart at 7, and sat on the beach smoking and discoursing with two German botanists till 9, when the steamer arrived. The ceremony of embarking was most perilous and provoking: we were utterly in the power of the negroes, who crammed six-and-twenty people into a boat not fit for more than twelve, and kept us nearly an hour in imminent danger of drowning. At last we got on board again and tried to go to sleep on deck, but half the passengers were drunk and the other half quarrelsome, and the coals were bad and the boilers foul, and the fireman had a boil in his armpit, so it was 4 o'clock A.M. before we got back to town, where we found the Governor's omnibus waiting for us.

On the 20th he was again under weigh in the 'Medway,' and on the 21st at Grenada, and after touching at Jacmel, in St. Domingo, on December 30th landed at Port Royal, in Jamaica, and on January 2, 1847, sailed for the Havana, which he reached on the 5th at 2 P.M., and where he saw the town illuminated in honour of the 'auspicious marriage'[1] of Isabella II., Queen of Spain, and attended a great ball given by the garrison, of which he writes: 'Women almost without exception hideous; supper excellent.' The journal gives the following unpleasant picture of an incident in the city of slaves.

February 4, 1847.—Coming home to-night, the streets being pretty full, there was a stoppage—a *volante* horse backed, and of course all the others behind him had to do the same. The last of all backed against a Spaniard who was crossing the street; the driver could not avoid doing so,

[1] 'El fausto enlace' is the Spanish phrase quoted in the journal. On October 10, 1846, the ex-Queen Isabella was married to her cousin Don Francisco de Assisi, and her sister, the Infanta Louisa, to the Duc de Montpensier; matches not now generally considered auspicious, though they will long be famous as the Spanish marriages of the nineteenth century.

neither could he see the Spaniard. The scoundrel borrowed a stick and commenced violently belabouring the poor nigger, who sat quite unmoved, though he was a fine muscular man, able to have eaten his assailant, and held in his hand a huge horsewhip. The bystanders rushed out, not to interfere or cry shame upon the Spaniard, but to incite him to give it well to the *volante* driver, and to exclaim loudly that had he driven against them they would have massacred him. It was a painful sight to see.

Having laid in a stock of cigars worth 70*l*., and having been honoured with special notice by Madame Cabanas, the chief manufacturer, who caused a 'cigar monstre' to be made in commemoration of his stature, he again sailed in the 'Medway' on February 11, and landed at Southampton on the 1st or 2nd of March, 1847.

His visits to the West Indies were of no inconsiderable advantage to Mr. Higgins. Having studied the social and economical problems of our sugar-growing colonies on the spot, he was able in future years to understand the interests, control the management, and maintain the productiveness of his estate, duties which absentee-proprietors are generally obliged to delegate to others, with results like those with which the owner of Affiance had to deal in 1838. His practical acquaintance with these colonies also served him in good stead as a public writer when colonial affairs became, as they afterwards did for some time, the frequent theme of his pen.

IV.

Soon after his return from Demerara, the Potato Famine, which desolated the south and west of Ireland in 1846 and 1847, was at its height. He immediately offered his services to the Relief Committee, and was for several months actively engaged in Ireland or in London in the good work of ministering to the necessities of the starving inhabitants of the north-western district of Connaught.

On April 7, he landed at Balmullet, on the coast of Mayo, from H.M.S. 'Terrible,' which had been sent thither with supplies. Balmullet was the chief village of the barony of Erris, in which the famine and the attendant pestilence raged with the most disastrous fury. Mayo was the most cruelly smitten of the Irish counties, and Erris was the most miserable part of Mayo. 'Afflicting as is the condition of Mayo,' said an eye-witness, 'there is a district almost as distinct from Mayo as Mayo is from the eastern part of Ireland. Human wretchedness seems to have culminated in Erris, and the culminating point of man's physical degradation to have been reached in the Mullet.'[1] If to 'physical' he had added moral 'degradation,' he would have hardly exceeded the truth as regards that part of the population which ought to have been least degraded. Erris is a promontory stretching into the Atlantic, forming part of the union of Ballina, a union 60 miles long by 30 miles wide, and at that time possessing only a single poor-house. The deeply indented shores were washed by waters abounding in fish, but 'there was not a wherry or fishing-smack in the entire barony!'[2] The population of Erris was estimated, before the famine, at 28,000 souls. Of these 2,000 are supposed to have emigrated to England, and 6,000 to have perished of starvation and fever. The landowners, all but two, were bankrupt in purse or in character, and of these two, one only gave any efficient aid. The middle-men, 'the useless drones, who squeezed the life-blood out of the miserable tenantry,'[3] of course did

[1] Report of James H. Tuke, in *Transactions of the Central Relief Committee of the Society of Friends* during the famine in Ireland, 1846–7. Dublin, 1852, 8vo, p. 205.

[2] *Letters on the Condition of the People of Ireland*, by T. Campbell Foster. London, 1847, 8vo, p. 218. He cites the 6th *Annual Report of Board of Public Works in Ireland*, p. 6.

[3] Foster's *Letters*, p. 396. Of the class of middle-men, the national hero O'Connell was one of the most unpleasant types, seeing that his administration of his property could be excused on the score neither of ignorance nor necessity. On this subject it may be

nothing; duty and charity being ideas beyond their conception. Men, women, and children, were dying daily, not only in the wretched cabins, but in the village streets and on the roadsides. Mr. Higgins and his associate Mr. Bynoe, a naval surgeon, were besieged at once for food, clothing, medicine, and coffins. They found it necessary to place the distribution of the funds and supplies provided by the Relief Committee in the hands of strangers, the locality affording no person sufficiently patriotic, intelligent, or honest to undertake or to be entrusted with the duty. No native could be discovered fit to manage a soup-kitchen; those who were willing to assist 'being,' as Mr. Higgins wrote, 'as incapable of comprehending the regulations issued by the Relief Committee as of making a watch.' Those from whom aid might have been expected were callous to the misery around them, or solicitous to turn the public calamity to their private advantage. When at last the local relief committee had got into working order, the greatest vigilance was required to prevent the resources

instructive to read Mr. Foster's remarks (pp. 395-7), O'Connell's long, abusive, and evasive reply (pp. 667-693), and Mr. Foster's rejoinder (pp. 521-552), passages from which may be obtained a picture of the 'Liberator' very different from those exhibited at the late Centenary at Dublin.

provided by British benevolence from being wasted on those who were comparatively well off; the supplies being, whenever it was possible, intercepted by the local gentry for their own dependents, and the money applied to the payment of wages which ought to have come out of their own pockets. The letters of Mr. Higgins written from Erris corroborated the complaints of the Relief Commissioners [1] of the absence of all local benevolence, the shiftlessness and idleness of the poor, the shameless applications for aid by the well-to-do, the frequent sale of food and clothing by those who had fraudulently obtained them, and the hopeless dishonesty of all classes. To the British public Mr. Higgins communicated his experience in the following letter, which appeared in the 'Times' of April 22nd, 1847:—

Sir,—It may be in the recollection of some of your readers, that when we City gentlemen were reviled last year by the 'noble country party' for the selfishness of our pursuits, and the inutility of our lives, as compared with those of deputy-lieutenants and county magistrates, I availed myself of your kindness to vindicate as well as I could in your columns the order to which it is my pride to belong.

[1] *Reports of the Relief Commissioners*, especially Nos. 5, 6, and 7, 1847.

Perhaps, however, the taunts of the landed aristocracy have not been entirely without their use. The Barings, the Rothschilds, the Jones Loyds, and other monied magnates of London, have at least since last year nobly borne their share in attempting to relieve famine-stricken Ireland ; and I have endeavoured to follow in their footsteps—*longo intervallo*, I admit.

The Committee of the British Association for the Relief of Distress in Ireland, reading frightful accounts of pestilence and famine in the county of Mayo, and receiving urgent and perplexing appeals for relief from various resident clergymen and landlords, decided on despatching one of their number to the spot, to examine into the state of affairs and relieve the people promptly. As I had been loudest in my condemnation of the conduct of both English and Irish landlords, and had boasted—I now feel somewhat injudiciously—of what I would do were I in their place, I was selected for this not very agreeable service. In consequence, I have been for the last few weeks resident in Letterbrick, the capital of the barony of Arderry. If you can spare me room in your columns, I purpose to lay before the public as accurate a sketch as I can draw of what is actually happening here.

The barony contains 185,000 acres of land, over which is scattered a population of 30,000 souls. The little town of Letterbrick is placed in the bight of a deep bay, one of the many noble harbours with which the west of Ireland abounds. The Union workhouse is 31 miles distant ; besides that, there is neither hospital nor dispensary of which the poor can avail themselves at the present moment.

Of three resident Protestant clergymen, one is insane ;

the other two are not on speaking terms, and will not 'act' together in any way.

The three Roman Catholic priests are good simple men— poor and ignorant, and possessing little influence over their flocks.

Two-thirds of this vast extent of land is divided between two proprietors—Mr. Black of Kildare, and The Mulligan, who resides in his baronial castle of Ballymulligan.

The Mulligan having been an Irish man of pleasure, is now a bankrupt ; he amuses himself in his dominions as well as he can, but has lately been cast in damages for the seduction of the daughter of a coast-guard, and is in consequence at present playing at hide-and-seek with the officers of the law : he is a married man ; he is the only resident magistrate in Arderry, and as his present discreditable social position renders him only accessible on Sundays, he is utterly useless in that capacity.

His tenants are not in arrear. They have been driven, ejected, and sold up with incredible severity. To give you an idea of what the people here endure and the landlords perpetrate, I will state that last week, accompanied by two credible English witnesses, I met several emaciated cows, driven by two men, and followed by their still more emaciated owners, proceeding towards Letterbrick.

I stopped them and inquired whither they were going. The two men said they were taking them to the Letterbrick pound for rent owing to them. The peasants declared that the rent was not due till the 1st of May. Their landlord admitted this readily ; but added, that Letterbrick fair was on the 12th of April, and he feared, unless he pounded his tenants' cattle before that, that they would sell them at the fair and be off to America. So he did pound them, for a debt that was not yet due; and the poor ignorant starved wretches allowed him to do it.

Of The Mulligan's exertions and charities to meet the present crisis, it is needless to speak. He is chairman of a relief committee, which he never attends; he has given no money or food, whilst he has extracted all he can from the soil. He pays no taxes, builds no cottages or farm buildings, supports no schools or hospitals. The only duties which he attempts to perform are those which he considers he owes to himself. He and his family own about 40,000 acres of land.

His uncle I saw when he came to propose to the purser on board the 'Horrible' steamer, in charge of a cargo of seed, to let him have some on the security of his 'paper at six months;' and when we were landing some meal in the rain from that vessel, his brother galloped into the town in a rickety tandem, pulled up to stare at us, and, after having played an amatory national air on a horn which he had slung round him, galloped off again.

Mr. Black, his co-proprietor, is a landlord of a very different species. He resides in Kildare, where he has a large property, and, by his own account, takes an active part in the duties of the county.

Here he is represented by his agent, Mr. White, a most intelligent and gentlemanlike young man, who spends a few months occasionally in Arderry, and is a magistrate.

I will not take the liberty of saying anything more of Mr. Black, as the correspondence which I have had with him will speak for itself. I append it to this letter.

A variety of small and sub-landlords, whose lives are spent in watching the growing crops and cattle of their tenants, and pouncing upon them the moment they are ripe or fit for sale, occupy the rest of the barony, and complete the misery of the people.

There is one single man who believes that he has duties to perform, and does his best to fulfil them ; but as his property is small, the good he can do is but as a drop in this ocean of human iniquity, and being a Dublin lawyer, he is necessarily an absentee.

At this moment there is no food in the country, save what is imported by Government and the British Association ; neither have the people any money, save what they earn on the public works, which are to be stopped in May.

The land is unsown,—there will be no harvest. The 'Horrible,' when she was here selling seed under prime cost, sold but 100*l.* worth, and that almost entirely to the benevolent individual I have alluded to. At Killala, where the gentry clamoured loudly for seed, the 'Lightning' was sent with 350 sacks, of which she sold *one* ; and at Killibegs the 'Horrible' had no better market.

There is at this moment, Sir, fever in half the houses in Arderry—I call them houses by courtesy, for they are but hollow, damp, and filthy dungheaps. The people sell their last rag for food, and are then forced to remain in their hovels until the weakest sink from hunger ; their festering corpses, which they have no means of removing, then breed a fever which carries off the rest.

Efficient medicines or medical aid they have none, and if they had, what but good food could be prescribed with success to a starving man? During the short time I have been here I have seen my fellow-creatures die in the streets. I have found the naked bodies of women on the road-side, and piles of coffins containing corpses left outside the cabins and in the market-place. I have met mothers carrying about dead infants in their arms until they were putrid, refusing to bury them, in the hope that the offensive sight might wring charity from the callous townspeople sufficient to protract for a while the lives of the other children at home. During the last two days I have buried at my own expense twenty bodies, which, had I not done so, would be still infecting the living.

I must here pause to remind you, Sir, that I am a man of business, deliberate and calculating, nowise given to exaggeration, and that what I am detailing to you is not the recollection of some horrid nightmare, but a state of society within two days' post of London.

The people here, naturally docile, become uncontrollable at the sight of provisions—not a bag of biscuit can be landed or leave the town without an armed escort, not a vessel can anchor in the bay without imminent risk of being plundered. Yesterday, three vessels, bound to the north, were becalmed off the coast; they were instantly boarded and cleared by the famished and desperate peasantry.

I purchased a little seed myself, which I retailed in small quantities to the people, chiefly to gain some insight into their position. I found them utterly hopeless, almost indifferent about sowing, because they are aware that any crops they may sow will be seized on for rent by the landlords. They preferred buying turnip and parsnip seed, although they appeared quite ignorant how to cultivate them, because the perishable nature of these roots renders them less convenient for seizure than barley or oats.

On my arrival here I found the soup-kitchen, on which the lives of hundreds depend, stopped, not for want of funds, but because the vicar and the curate, having 130*l.* intrusted to them jointly by our Association, had quarrelled, and preferred seeing the parishioners starve to making soup for them in concert.

Lest I may be suspected of caricature or exaggeration, I will, in conclusion, set down what my eyes have seen during the last half-hour.

I have seen in the court-house an inquest holding on the body of a boy of 13, who, being left alone in a cabin, with a little rice and fish in his charge, was murdered by his cousin, a boy of 12, for the sake of that wretched pittance of food. A verdict of 'Wilful Murder' has since been returned.

The culprit is the most famished and sickly little creature I ever saw, and his relatives whom I heard examined were all equally emaciated and fever-stricken.

Driven from the court by the stench of the body, I passed in the street two coffins with bodies in them, in going to my lodgings from the court-house, a distance of a hundred yards. I am prepared to hear that the truth of what I have here stated has been impugned; to be informed that I am ignorant of the habits of the people, and that I have been humbugged by Irishmen having a natural turn for humour. I am prepared to be ridiculed for my obesity, and to be told that a London banker is out of his element in the romantic regions of the west. I should not wonder if The Mulligan called me out. I feel certain 'he will court an inquiry.'

To all this I will answer, that to the truth of all I have here stated I can, fortunately, produce credible English witnesses; that if people have attempted to humbug me in the midst of the horrors which surround us, the less they boast of their mistimed humour the better; that by showing that I am ungracefully corpulent, and an indifferent snipe shot, they will not prove themselves to be humane landlords; and if The Mulligan exhibits any leaning towards the duello, I will inform him that, although constitutionally timid, I can take care of myself very well—having taken the precaution before I left London to borrow from an American friend, who is under some pecuniary obligations to our house, an excellent pair of Colt's revolvers—weapons, I believe, altogether new in the west of Ireland, but which are as effective in the hands of a flaccid cockney as in the grasp of the most sinewy descendant of Brian Boru that ever bounded barefoot over a bog.

I need scarcely say, Sir, that there is no such barony as Arderry in the west—no such town as Letterbrick—no such chieftain as The Mulligan of Ballymulligan—no such people as Messrs. Black and White; but there are a barony, a town, and people exactly like them, who are acting exactly in the manner I have described. If they court an inquiry, they shall have every facility given them by me for it. I will supply names, dates, and places, if they wish me to do so.

I will only observe, that the day before I left town, just after I read the debate about Captain Wynne's case, in which Mr. Labouchere made such a manly and creditable answer to

Major Macnamara,[1] my pocket was picked in the street. I caught a boy who I fancied was the culprit, and handed him over to letter B 27. The lad exhibited the most virtuous indignation, exclaiming, 'Search me, and you will find that I am innocent!' He courted an inquiry. The matter-of-fact policeman took him at his word, and, lo! my handkerchief was found in his possession. I have therefore inferred, that courting an inquiry when you see that it will be made whether you court it or not, is not always a proof of innocence.

I have the honour to remain, Sir,

Your faithful servant,

JACOB OMNIUM.

April 18.

ENCLOSURE No. 1.

'*Jacob Omnium, Agent for the British Association for the Relief of the destitute Irish, to W. H. Black, Esq., Kildare.*

' Sir,—Having been commissioned by the British Association to accompany Mr. Squills, R.M., a surgeon deputed by Government for the same purpose to Letterbrick, in Her Majesty's ship " Horrible," conveying a cargo of seed to Mayo and Donegal, and to report to them the actual state of the people and the exertions which were being made by the landed proprietors to save them, I feel it my painful duty

---

[1] On March 23, 1847, Mr. C. O'Brien moved in the House of Commons, Major Macnamara seconding the motion, for a Committee to inquire into the conduct and statements of Captain Wynne, Inspecting Officer under the Board of Works, employed in

to call your attention to the miserable tenantry on your estates in Arderry.

'They are daily dying from sheer famine, and rotting in the cabins where they die.

'They have none to look to for aid; for if you, who have for many years derived your resources from hence, abandon those whose labour has supplied those resources the moment they cease to be profitable to you for a time, you cannot expect that the charity of England can be extended to the tenants of men who themselves will not bestir themselves to save them.

'Your agent, Mr. White, aware of the arrival of the "Horrible," and of the cargo which she brought, left Arderry the day she anchored in the bay, without making any arrangements for procuring seed for your people, and there is now no one in the country to represent your extensive property here, or even to bear, personally, any share in the arduous task of dispensing the funds which English public and private charity may devote to the relief of the diseased and starving poor on your estates.

Clare in November and December 1846. These gentlemen were the members for Clare of whom Captain Wynne had complained, in an official letter, that they had attended a public meeting 'apparently for the purpose of holding us up one and all to assassination, and hallooing on a mob,' &c. On the part of Captain Wynne, Mr. Labouchere said that that officer 'never intended to impute to them designedly the purpose of assassination;' and he generally defended Captain Wynne's character and his good service in a very trying position. Hansard's *Parl. Debates*, March 23, 1847; cols. 326–332.

'I earnestly request that you will, without delay, do me the honour of acquainting me whether you are prepared to co-operate in any way with the British Association in saving the lives of the dying poor on your lands.

'I am, Sir, your obedient humble servant,
'JACOB OMNIUM,
'Agent to the British Association.

'Letterbrick, April 11, 1847.
'W. H. Black, Esq., Kildare.'

To this letter Mr. Black returned an answer, saying that he had for twenty years watched anxiously over and devoted large sums of money to his tenantry in Arderry; that his agent was a most able and respectable man, and did not deserve my censure; that it was evident I had written my letter hastily; that his own age and duties in Kildare prevented his attending personally to his estates in Arderry, but that Mr. White would immediately return furnished with powers to co-operate with me in every practicable manner. Mr. Black further informed me that for the last two years he had *not received a farthing from his property here*, and that the Government measures—amounting in his opinion to a confiscation of his estate—prevented his going to any expense about it.

This I believe to be a fair *précis* of his letter. I have sent it to London, and cannot, therefore, publish it now; but if he thinks I have garbled it, I will do so whenever he pleases.

ENCLOSURE No. 2.

'*Jacob Omnium to W. H. Black, Esq.*

'Sir,—If you will re-read the letter which I had the honour of addressing you, you will see that I made no reflections whatever either on the manner in which you had thought fit to conduct your estates in Arderry in past years, or on the conduct of your agent, of whom I knew nothing, save that he had made no arrangements for availing himself of the facilities which the Government and the British Association had afforded you for supplying your tenants with seed.

'I have just had an interview with him. He freely admits that the high price of provisions has rendered your tenants penniless, that they are daily dying of starvation, and that the only instructions he has received from you are to confine his expenditure for their relief to any sums he may henceforward wring from them.

'He corroborates the information which I had already received, that this town and about 60,000 acres of land, with a population of 12,000 souls, belong to you at a rent-roll of 2,500*l.* a year, part of which is from a year to a year and a half in arrear; that in 1846 a sum of 70*l.* was expended on your account in labour for your own benefit; and that since January 1st your charities over your entire property here are comprised in the sum of 15*l.*, granted to the soup-kitchen of Letterbrick.

'Yesterday, at my own private expense, I had the bodies of four of your tenants drawn out of their cabins, where they were breeding fever and pestilence, placed in coffins, and buried. Their wretched relatives had no money to purchase coffins, and were too weak to carry them to the grave.

'Mr. White, since his return, has met one of your people carrying on his back to the burial-ground the corpse of his wife stuffed into a fish basket.

'As you have supplied him with no funds, he can do nothing to alleviate this horrid misery; and as you are not disposed to provide seed for your tenants, unless the English support them—not till harvest, for there will be no harvest, but for an indefinite period—they must all die. I thank Heaven that I am here upon the spot to bear witness to and publish a state of things which I could not have believed possible in a Christian country.

'I am, Sir, your obedient servant,

'JACOB OMNIUM,

'Agent to the British Association.

'W. H. Black, Esq., April 16.'

Subsequently to my sending letter No. 2, Mr. White called upon me and mentioned that Mr. Black had, in addition to the 70*l.* disbursed in 1846, spent 200*l.* on his estate that year; but that since January he had, as I have stated, contributed but 15*l.* to meet the present crisis. He further said that Mr. Black did *not clear more than* 1,000*l. last year out of the property.*

The class of which types were thus pourtrayed under the pseudonyms of 'The O'Mulligan' and 'Mr. Black' was largely represented in the House of Commons.

The mild statement of Mr. Labouchere, the Irish Secretary, that 'Government had not received the support which it had a right to expect from the gentry of Ireland,'[1] was received with so much noisy indignation by some of the Irish members, that Mr. Roebuck was justified in the remark that some of them 'seemed to think it the first and great duty of the people of England to feed, clothe, and shave them.'[2] These patriots scouted the idea that any gratitude was due to the sister-kingdoms for sums voted by Parliament and subscribed by the public for the relief of Irish distress, and some of them imputed the basest motives to their benefactors. One of them was not ashamed to tell the House of Commons that those who stated plain facts showing the supineness of Irish landlords during the pressure of the famine 'were hunting them to death in order that English capitalists might step in and buy up their estates, and so invest their money in Irish land.'[3] It would be painful to recur to many of the events and

[1] *Annual Register*, 1847: History, p. 32. Hansard, 1847, January 19, c. 692.
[2] *Annual Register*: History, p. 30. Hansard, 1847, Feb. 1, c. 653.
[3] *Annual Register*: History, p. 35. Hansard, 1847, Feb. 8, c. 457-8.

speeches of that trying time, were it not for the cheering evidence of more recent history that the faults of his countrymen which Mr. Higgins was compelled to expose are in course of amendment. The Irishmen of 1847 were very angry with Lord John Russell for exhorting them to adopt the maxim 'Help yourselves and Heaven will help you;'[1] but the lessons of the famine have not been wholly lost, even upon the generation which listens to the Fenian rebel and the agitator for Home Rule.

V.

On the retirement of Sir Robert Peel from the helm of public affairs in 1846, and the schism in the Conservative party of which the repeal of the Corn Laws was the occasion, some members of the late Cabinet endeavoured to organise a separate political connection, professing Conservative opinions but remaining distinct from the Protectionists led by Lord Derby and Mr. Disraeli, the Whigs whose chief was Lord John Russell, and the Radicals who followed Mr. Cobden and Mr. Bright. Mr. Higgins had up to this time been a Con-

---

[1] *Annual Register*, 1847: History, p. 47. Hansard, 1847, Jan. 25, c. 452.

servative, though without having taken any active part in politics, or formed any close tie to party. Many of the new political sect were his personal friends, and he not unnaturally fell into its ranks.

At the General Election of 1847 Mr. Higgins addressed the electors of Westbury, and stood for that borough on Peelite principles; but he was defeated by Mr. James Wilson, afterwards Financial Secretary of the Treasury and Finance Minister in India, by a majority of twenty-one. In a characteristic letter written during the contest, he described his opponent as an 'unpleasantly clever fellow.' He never again was a candidate for a seat in Parliament, though his interest in public affairs continued unabated, and there were few figures more familiar than his own in the lobby or under the gallery of the House of Commons, or near the bar of the House of Lords.

The 'Morning Chronicle,' the once famous organ of the Whigs during their long exclusion from office and their early and palmy days of power, had about this time been overtaken by some of those chances and changes of journalistic life by which flourishing periodicals are minished and brought low, and finally, with a shattered reputation, into the market. The more ambitious and wealthy supporters of Sir Robert Peel were in want of a newspaper at the time that the proprietors of the 'Morning Chronicle' were seeking for a purchaser. A bargain was struck, as was commonly believed, with Mr. Sidney Herbert, afterwards Lord Herbert of Lea, and the late Duke of Newcastle; and early in 1848 the 'Morning Chronicle' became the organ of what began to be called the Peel party. It was conducted with great vigour and ability by Mr. J. D. Cook, and was supported by the leading politicians and men of letters who wore the colours of Sir Robert Peel. Mr. Higgins was one of the most important accessions to the cause, and one of the chief writers in the 'Chronicle.' With his friend Mr. John Robert Godley[1] he took charge of its colonial department. Their sharp skirmishes with the Colonial Office under Lord Grey during the government of Lord John Russell, attracted much attention, and are possibly still remembered by those whom they concerned. Notwithstanding the remarkable talent and spirit with which the 'Chronicle' was conducted, its brilliant leaders, its

---

[1] *Selections from the Writings and Speeches of John Robert Godley*, collected and arranged by J. E. Fitzgerald. New Zealand, Christchurch, 1863, 8vo, Memoir, p. 8.

excellent foreign correspondence, and the searching manner with which it dealt with many important social questions at home, it never became a commercial success. As a party organ its basis was too narrow; every man's pen not enlisted in the cause was against the party which sought, according to the phrase of a later time, 'to dish the Whigs' by adopting their principles while repudiating their name. The Peelites did good service in their day; witness their protest against the stupid Ecclesiastical Titles Act, passed by the Whigs with the aid of the Tories, an Act which its authors never dared to enforce, which never was enforced, and which was repealed some sixteen years afterwards without a dissentient voice. But the exigencies of political life compelled its members to ally themselves with one or other of the divisions of the Liberal camp; and the formation of the Aberdeen Government, in which its leaders were included, destroyed its separate existence, and probably achieved the main objects for which the 'Chronicle' had been bought. That paper, after entailing heavy loss on individual proprietors, was sold at a very low rate in 1854, and after lingering for a few years died of exhaustion and discredit.

In 1850 (July 2) Mr. Higgins married Emily Blanche,

daughter of Sir Henry Joseph Tichborne of Tichborne, and widow of the eldest son of Mr. Benett of Pythouse, Wiltshire. After his marriage he removed from No. 1 Lowndes Square, where he had lived for some years, to No. 71 Eaton Square, to a house of which a wide circle of friends still retain many pleasant social reminiscences. During the summer and autumn Mr. and Mrs. Higgins resided for some years at Pythouse, the property of her son by her former marriage, until, at the youth's death in 1856, the estate passed into other hands.

VI.

For many years Mr. Higgins was a constant contributor to the 'Times,' chiefly as a writer of letters on all kinds of questions, political and municipal, civil and military, grave and gay. 'Jacob Omnium,' 'J. O.,' 'Civilian,' 'Paterfamilias,' 'West Londoner,' 'Belgravian Mother,' 'Mother of Six,' 'A Thirsty Soul,' 'John Barleycorn,' and 'Providus,' were only a few of the names under which he wrote. His graver and more important letters were generally signed 'J. O.' It was under the name of 'Civilian' that he attacked the

Purchase System, and anticipated many of the changes which have since received the sanction of Parliament. As 'Paterfamilias' he opened the eyes of, and spread rage and dismay amongst, the sleepy authorities of our fashionable public schools; he led the van in the discussions out of which the Public Schools Commission arose; and he may be justly credited with the removal of many of the blots and abuses which disfigured the schools at which the children of the wealthy acquired their small Latin and less Greek.

These names were not assumed by Mr. Higgins for the purpose of concealment or mystification, nor did he ever make a secret of the authorship of his writings. His clear and trenchant style soon revealed him to his readers, and the voice of 'Jacob' was detected under each new disguise, almost as soon as it was put on. For the 'Edinburgh,' and other Reviews, he wrote various excellent articles, and to the 'Cornhill Magazine' he was a frequent contributor, generally under one or other of his favourite signatures. Some of these were occasionally collected and reprinted as pamphlets, of which a list will be found at the end of this notice. For his friends he reprinted privately in 1857 some of his early magazine articles, together with a few essays apparently written at an earlier date but now printed for the first time, entitling the volume 'Social Sketches.'

The long connection of Mr. Higgins and the 'Times' was brought to an end soon after the conclusion of the famous court-martial on Lieut.-Colonel Crawley of the 6th or Inniskilling Dragoons, which sat at Aldershot in the autumn of 1863. That court-martial arose out of another held at Mhow in India in April and June 1862, on Captain and Paymaster Smales of the same regiment, at which Sergeant-Major Lilley had been an important witness for the defence. Placed under close arrest by his colonel, Sergeant-Major Lilley and his wife died under circumstances which aroused strong sympathy and indignation both in India and at home. During the session of 1863 the case was frequently brought under the notice of the House of Commons, and was the subject of endless writing in the newspapers. The 'Times' pronounced strongly against Colonel Crawley. In its columns the proceedings of the court-martial at Mhow were severely criticised by Mr. Higgins, and the authorities at the Horse Guards were persistently attacked for permitting, or for not punishing, what was alleged to have been cruel injustice to Sergeant-Major Lilley. In Parliament and the press Colonel

Crawley found few persons or pens disposed to take his part. It is not too much to say that Mr. Higgins and the 'Times' were the most prominent combatants in the assault on the Horse Guards which led to the court-martial at Aldershot. The November number of the 'Cornhill Magazine' contained an article from his pen entitled 'The Story of the Mhow Court-martial,' in which the report presented to Parliament was epitomised in his usual masterly style. By the friends of Colonel Crawley the article was strongly condemned, as tending to prejudice the tribunal and the public against the accused; while to others it appeared that the Smales court-martial and its published proceedings were matters of history, which were of great public interest at that moment, and which it was therefore open to any writer to examine and discuss.

Whatever may be the view which an impartial critic would now take of the Crawley case and the cases connected with it, there can be no doubt that, during the protracted sitting of the court-martial at Aldershot, and after its verdict, the tide of public opinion, hitherto adverse to the defendant, began to turn, and ended by setting strongly in his favour. It was obvious that much exaggeration had prevailed, and that a good deal of incredible testimony had been given on both sides; but the general result of the evidence was hostile to the conclusions of the 'Times.' The defence of Colonel Crawley and the reply of the Public Prosecutor appeared in the 'Times' on December 18 and 19, 1863.[1] On Monday, December 21, a leading article announced that an 'admirable defence and an admirable reply' enabled the public to review the whole case, which the writer accordingly proceeded to review in a style which left it doubtful to which side his nicely adjusted balance inclined.[2] On December 24 the finding of the court-martial, 'full and honourable acquittal,' was published,[3] and the opposite page of the 'Times' contained an article in which its previous opinions were retracted, not only with a flourish of trumpets, but also with a volley of musketry fired in the faces of those who had hitherto followed its lead. 'In the meantime,' these were the concluding words of the article, 'it is for the authors of the cruel slanders which have cost the country this vast expense, and their victim such unmerited obloquy, to stand on their own defence; and for those who believed them to make the only reparation

---

[1] *Times*, Dec. 18 and 19, 1863, pp. 4 and 12.
[2] *Times*, Dec. 21, pp. 8, 9.   [3] *Times*, Dec. 24, p. 9.

in their power by expressing, without reserve, their sense of the injustice which has been done.'[1] Mr. Higgins remained of the opinion that whatever unmerited obloquy had been cast on Colonel Crawley, Sergeant-Major Lilley had died the victim of cruel and unredressed injustice. He likewise knew that if slander there had been, he and the 'Times' had been amongst the chief slanderers. He therefore accepted the challenge, and in an elaborate letter, signed 'J. O.' and dated Paris, December 30, stated his reasons for dissenting from the verdict. This letter was admitted with extreme reluctance, and not till January 12, 1864.[2] It was followed next day by a severe reply signed 'Verax,'[3] to which no rejoinder was allowed. The result was a correspondence between Mr. Higgins and the proprietor of the 'Times,' which, having been privately printed, is a curiosity of literature. The third letter in the series was the last which Mr. Higgins addressed to Printing House Square. That nothing could come of such an appeal he might have foreseen, and his own observation should have taught him that timely retreat from any unpopular opinion was the habit and the policy

---

[1] *Times*, Dec. 24, 1863, p. 8.   [2] *Times*, Jan. 12, 1864, p. 6.
[3] *Times*, Jan. 13, 1864, p. 5.

of the 'Times.' But the incident, nevertheless, caused him much surprise and pain, and led him to renounce some old and valued friendships.

During the remainder of his life his contributions to daily literature were made almost exclusively to the 'Pall Mall Gazette.' The name of that journal was suggested by the famous newspaper which figures in Thackeray's 'Pendennis,' and its convenient form, handsome type, and attractive paper, were improvements on the ways of the press which Mr. Higgins highly applauded. The 'Occasional Notes,' which also formed a distinctive feature of the new periodical, were well adapted to display the special qualities of his pen. His keen sense of humour enabled him to select the tit-bits of the day's intelligence, and his neat style and light and nimble hand, to set them before the reader in the most dainty fashion. 'Occasional Notes' are now found in most newspapers; but the copies often differ from the original, as *plats* of Paris from dishes with like names at Richmond and Greenwich.

His connection with the Tichborne family led Mr. Higgins to take much interest in the famous case of the disputed Tichborne succession. In the earlier stages of that celebrated plea he took an active part in examining and exposing the claims of the butcher from Wapping and Australia, now expiating his perjuries at Dartmoor.

In the spring of 1865, having spent the winter at Nice, he paid a visit to Corsica and Sardinia, of which a letter dated Oristano, March 15, gave his impressions, and may serve as a specimen of his epistolary style:—

'On the 8th I started from Nice with a Director of the Royal Sardinian Railway, who was desirous of seeing with his own eyes what the prospects of that undertaking really are. It is to connect the N.W. and N.E. points of Sardinia with the capital, Cagliari, at the southern extremity of the island. We first went to Bastia, in Corsica, whence we had intended to cross the island to Ajaccio, and join the Marseilles boat there to Porto Torres in Sardinia. But a heavy fall of rain cut off all communication between Bastia and Ajaccio, and, after waiting a couple of days at Bastia, we got on board a small boat from Leghorn, which touches at Bastia on its way to Porto Torres. The weather was horribly bad, and the steamer very weak, and we were forced to take refuge in the Maddalenas. While waiting there we took the opportunity of paying Garibaldi a visit at Caprera, and were very hospitably received by that potentate and his sons. He is living there very simply and comfortably, and he has chosen a charming retreat, as like the Scilly Islands as one place can be to another. The next day we started afresh, and after a very rough twenty-four hours in a very frail and crazy boat, we landed at the N.W. corner of Sardinia. We have been employed for the last three days in working our way down to this town, and to-morrow night we shall reach Cagliari. The whole of Sardinia that I have yet seen is exactly like what the worst parts of Ireland were thirty years ago, save that there is little or no population. In ninety miles we have only met one carriage; we have passed but one small town and two villages, and have literally not seen one other human habitation of any kind. The whole country appears to be given up to flocks of goats and sheep and herds of cattle and horses, and by far the greatest portion of the line will pass through a howling wilderness of granite and lava. I really did not believe such a place existed. The town in which we are staying to-night, Oristano, is sixty miles from Cagliari, and they tell us the country we shall pass through to-morrow is better cultivated and more fertile than what we have yet seen; but it is just at present under water from the overflowing of the river here, the Tirso, which they are momentarily expecting to enter the town, and, as the houses are chiefly built of unburnt bricks, if it does, we shall dissolve like lump-sugar. However, I have great hopes it will defer the dissolution of the city till we start to-morrow. The consternation of my travelling companion at the aspect of the country through which he has been induced to carry 250 miles of railway is indescribable. There are only between 400,000 and 500,000 inhabitants in the island, and these almost exclusively of the lowest class. In the country there are literally none above the class who ride about at the tail of a flock of sheep or a drove of horses with a gun at their backs, and no gentry of any kind or degree. So it is difficult to conceive who is to travel by the railway, or what articles of commerce are to be sent by it. The inns on the way hither are of a lower class as to the accommodation they afford than the lowest shebeen house in Connemara or Erris. Meat and drink they had none to offer, and had we not been under the charge and guidance of the engineer and contractor of the railway, we should have fared very sadly. The weather too, has, been very bad.

During his later years Mr. Higgins sometimes complained of flagging health, and paid annual visits to the baths of Homburg without deriving much benefit from their waters. But no failure of physical or intellectual vigour was discernible by his friends ; he continued to be an early riser, and to fulfil his literary and social engagements with exact regularity, and even in his own family no cause for anxiety was perceived. In the autumn of 1868 he was taken ill after bathing at Kingston House, near Abingdon ; and, after a confinement of six days, died there on the evening of August 14. Seven days afterwards, on the 21st, he was buried near his younger son in the Roman Catholic Cemetery at Fulham.

His widow survives him. They had four children, of whom three are living: Mary Alicia ; Emily Blanche, married on May 2, 1872, to Charles, eldest son of C. R. Scott Murray, of Danesfield, Bucks ; and Henry Vincent, born April 18, 1855. A second son, Francis, died in infancy in 1858.

VII.

Mr. Higgins was certainly one of the most effective and popular public writers of his time. A letter from 'J. O.' was seldom left unread even by the most butterfly ranger over the newspapers. His peculiar gift of clear and concise statement was, as he used to relate, first revealed to himself by a happy accident. A friend dining next him at a Club, and being dissatisfied with the cooking or service of his dinner, appealed to his neighbour for sympathy. Thinking the complaint just, Mr. Higgins advised that it should be submitted in writing to the Committee, of which he himself was a member, and promised to support it at the next meeting. The ill-used diner called for pen and paper, but found none of several attempts to state adequately represented his wrongs. Mr. Higgins, taking the pen, soon drew up a brief and lucid narrative which not only satisfied the complainant, but obtained the applause of the Committee as a model of clear and temperate remonstrance. 'I never read so good a complaint,' said the Chairman; and on the author saying that he saw nothing very extraordinary in it, it was put into his hand with the further remark, 'Well, read it again, and tell me if you think you could have done it half as well yourself.'

A writer who made criticism of men and their doings his vocation, who could grasp a case firmly and state it clearly, and who possessed a pungent wit and incisive style, could not fail to make enemies of those whose policy he attacked and whose faults or blunders he exposed. His quiet and easy skill of fence often proved too much for the temper of his adversaries, and drew from them screams of rage which added to the delight of those who looked on. But as he never espoused a cause without a careful study of its facts and a thorough belief in its justice, he also pleased at least as many persons as he offended, and made many fast friends. Oppression or unfair dealing, whenever it came under his notice, was almost sure to bring 'J. O.' to the rescue. It would be absurd to pretend that in all his encounters with what he deemed to be wrong he was always wholly in the right; but it is not too much to say that no selfish object ever stimulated or stayed his pen. He had his reward in knowing that his labours for the public good were not in vain, and in seeing some things done which he had been among the first to indicate as things which ought to be attempted. Endeavours of his, in great things and small, of which he did not live to see the results, are now bearing fruit. Those who overthrew the purchase of commissions in the British army used but few arguments which will not be found marshalled in his writings. The British parent may thank him for certain improvements in our schools, for advocating which 'J. O.' was so severely chastised by the British schoolmaster. The horses of London, whose part he took in so many ways, benefit by his efforts to obtain the introduction of the steam-roller, which had long smoothed the path of their fellow-labourers in Paris.

In character and disposition Mr. Higgins was the reverse of the cynic which some of his literary antagonists used to paint him. His manners were very cordial, and his voice remarkable for its winning sweetness. It was fortunate for a man of his unusual stature, who could not enter a room or hardly be in a crowd without attracting especial notice, that nature had endowed him with a countenance of singular comeliness, intelligence, and benignity. Some of those who may read these pages will remember his pleasant and imposing aspect as he paced along Rotten Row, mounted on his tall bay horse—'le merveilleux cob' of the tall Englishman, for which the 'corpulent capitalist' proposed to treat on such advantageous terms after seeing the performance of both at Compiègne. (See 'Essays,' p. 212.) His Saul-like height was a frequent subject of his pleasant humour. His journal records how it was remarked of him at Grenada by one negress, 'Il est voyant le maître;' and by another, 'Massa him fill 'um eye.' He was in no wise displeased by his own caricatured likeness which his friend the inimitable Richard Doyle introduced into the supper room of his 'At Home, small and early,'[1] a figure which gives at least a just idea of his towering stature. He was delighted with the small urchin, who, carrying a load, first pushed against his knee, and then rebuked him with shrill displeasure: 'Now, then, can't you mind where you're a-going, you great overgrown beggar?' With Thackeray, likewise a tall man, he went to see a show giant. At the door, Thackeray pointed to his companion and whispered to the door-keeper, 'We are in the profession;' and so obtained free admission. 'But,' as Thackeray used to end the story, 'we were not mean, but paid our shillings as we came out.'

---

[1] *Bird's-eye View of Society*, by Richard Doyle. London 1864, obl. 4to, plate i. Mr. Higgins is just within the open door leading to the staircase.

In spite of his polemical habits, Mr. Higgins was, as he deserved to be, a social favourite. He talked, as he wrote, with point and terseness; related an anecdote well; and the delicate humour which pervaded his writings flavoured his conversation. There were few pursuits which found favour with English gentlemen with which he had not some acquaintance or sympathy. He loved literature, art, society, politics, and sport. He was equally at home at the auction rooms of Messrs. Christie and Manson, and in the yard and stables of Messrs. Tattersall; and at both places his taste and judgment were acknowledged. Many there are who still remember the pleasant well-assorted little dinners, both of his bachelor days and of his later life; and a few will have agreeable recollections of his breakfasts to the Philobiblon Society; or of those rarer Derby-day breakfasts, at which half-a-dozen friends, agreeing perhaps in nothing but good-fellowship, used to meet for the great summer holiday. Amongst those who, like their host, are now no more, and whose memories are associated with those Derby breakfasts, are Thackeray, Sir John Simeon, Sir Edwin Landseer, John Leech, and Count de Montalembert. Mr. Higgins formed the centre of a large and various circle, embracing men of all sorts of tastes, pursuits, and opinions.

An original member of the Cosmopolitan Club, he might have been taken as the best specimen of those whom its founders desired to form their society. A stranger in London could have found few better advisers or guides, and few persons more willing to take trouble in doing kindness. Busy as he was, he was ever ready to prove himself a friend in need, a counsellor in difficulty, a comforter in affliction. His long practice in weighing evidence enabled him often to mediate in disputes; and though in his literary vocation he was a man of many controversies, in his private capacity he was the author of not a few reconciliations.

The following Essays were, with few exceptions, collected by Mr. Higgins himself into a small volume, printed by him for private circulation in 1857, under the title of 'Social Sketches.' Most of them were written from thirty to forty years ago, and some of them describe things and ways unknown to the present generation. 'The Courier,' whose person, duties, and habits are so vividly sketched for us, is as much a being of the past as one of Cromwell's Ironsides; and even 'A Day with the Emperor's Hounds' at Compiègne presents a picture of life beyond the great gulf formed by the war of 1870. These are trifles only presenting one side of Mr. Higgins' mind, the social and humorous side; but of that they give a pleasant impression : and they may be read with interest by the new generation. If this belief should prove well founded, this volume may be followed by another consisting of specimens of Mr. Higgins' style in handling the minor public topics of the day.

The portrait prefixed to this volume is from a photograph taken in 1859 by Kilburn. In the possession of Mrs. Higgins there are two other portraits of her husband. One by Sir Francis Grant, P.R.A., a small full-length painted in 1861, represents him in profile, standing, looking at a picture placed on an easel; at his feet frisks a black-and-tan toy terrier, added to the composition by Sir Edwin Landseer. An admirable picture and likeness; it is reproduced in photography for these pages. The other portrait is an excellent life-size head in crayons, by Mr. Reginald Cholmondeley.

LIST OF THE WRITINGS OF MATTHEW JAMES HIGGINS, ISSUED IN A SEPARATE FORM DURING HIS LIFE.

Published.

Is Cheap Sugar the Triumph of Free Trade? A Letter to the Right Hon. Lord John Russell. By Jacob Omnium. London (James Ridgway), 1847, pp. 19.

Is Cheap Sugar the Triumph of Free Trade? A Second Letter to the Right Hon. Lord John Russell. By Jacob Omnium. London (James Ridgway), 1848, pp. 64.

A Third Letter to Lord John Russell, containing some Remarks on the Ministerial Speeches delivered during the late Sugar Debates; with an Appendix, containing Copies of the Despatches of Sir C. Grey and Lord Harris. By Jacob Omnium. London, (James Ridgway), 1848, pp. 41.

Cheap Sugar means Cheap Slaves. Speech of The Right Reverend The Lord Bishop of Oxford in the House of Lords, February 7, 1848, against the admission of Slave-labour Sugar on equal term with Free-labour Produce; with an Appendix illustrative of the impetus given to the Slave Trade by the Bill of 1846. Second edition. London (James Ridgway), 1848, pp. 32.

The Real Bearings of the West India Question, as expounded by the Most Intelligent and Independent Free-Trader of the day. Edited by Jacob Omnium, and dedicated to the Right Hon. Lord John Russell. London (James Ridgway), 1848, pp. 58.

Light Horse. By Jacob Omnium. London (Ridgway), 1855, 8vo. pp. 47. Reprinted from the *Times*, March 1855.

A Letter on Administrative Reform. By Jacob Omnium. London (M. S. Rickerby), 1855, pp. 7. Reprinted from the *Times*.

Letters on Military Education. By Jacob Omnium. Reprinted from the *Times*, and published during the Parliamentary Recess of 1855-56. London (Bradbury and Evans), 12mo. pp. viii. 155.

Letters on the Purchase System. By Jacob Omnium. London (Bradbury and Evans), 1857, 12mo. pp. 89.

Three Letters to the Editor of the Cornhill Magazine on Public School Education. By Paterfamilias. London (Smith, Elder and Co.), 1861, 8vo. pp. 78.

The Story of the Mhow Court Martial, with Notes and an Appendix. By J. O. Reprinted from the *Cornhill Magazine* of November 1863. London (Smith, Elder and Co.), 1864, 8vo. pp. iv. 80.

Papers on Public School Education in England in 1860. By Paterfamilias (M. J. Higgins). Reprinted from the *Cornhill Magazine* and *Edinburgh Review*. London (Smith, Elder and Co.), 1865, 8vo. pp. ii. 134.

Privately Printed.

Social Sketches. By M. J. H. London, printed by Bradbury and Evans, 1856. 12mo. title and contents and pp. 116.

Correspondence between J. Walter, Esq., M.P., and J. O. (M. Higgins, Esq.) [Westminster, printed by T. Brettell and Co., 1864], 8vo. pp. 18.

ESSAYS ON SOCIAL SUBJECTS.

JACOB OMNIUM, THE MERCHANT PRINCE.

MANY YEARS AGO, on leaving college, I took chambers in the Temple, where I was supposed by my father, who held a civil appointment in Ceylon, to be studying the law. Having no connections in town, or indeed any friends, save those whom I had made at Oxford, I fell into the society of some idle, dissipated, pleasant fellows, in circumstances nearly similar to my own.

We did not live extravagantly, for we had not the means of doing so; but, during the summer, we spent most of our leisure in an eight-oar on the river, and during the winter we amused ourselves, less innocently, by frequenting the theatres and gambling houses of the metropolis. I need scarcely add that we read but little.

Soon after I came to town I was introduced by one of my friends, or rather accomplices, to a low 'hell' in Bury Street, St. James's. It was conducted by two brothers named Jones. The game played was 'roulette,' and the stakes ranged from a shilling to a pound. Its frequenters were a shabby-looking set of elderly nondescripts, who all appeared to entertain a very favourable opinion of the proprietors of the establishment; whilst, on their part, the two hell-keepers, being well aware that in the due course of time the chances of the game in their favour would inevitably transfer all the money on the table into their pockets, were satisfied to await the regular course of events without attempting to accelerate it by any unfair exercise of legerdemain, which might, if discovered, disgust their patrons. Honesty was their best policy.

I was very young then. I had little money to lose, and do not now recollect whether the balance of my puny speculations at the 'Tally-ho Club' were in my favour or otherwise. Luckily, I had no real taste for play, and frequented the house chiefly for the sake of chatting with the elder Jones, who was a shrewd, entertaining fellow, and used to amuse me by recounting the various ingenious rascalities with which a twenty years' intimacy with the sporting circles of London had amply stored his mind.

We became great friends. Jones, hearing that the famous Temple eight-oar, the Beauséant, in which I pulled stroke, went up the river almost every day, begged me to call on him at his villa at Putney any Sunday I might happen to be there. I did so on the first opportunity, and he persuaded me to remain and dine with him and his daughter.

Zero Lodge was one of the first built of those little Elizabethan snuggeries with which the suburbs of London now abound. It stood in the centre of about four acres of ground, into which its projector had contrived to crowd a sort of parody on the luxurious accessories of a well-appointed country-seat. There was a fish-pond, a conservatory, a summer-house, a pheasantry, a dog-kennel, an excellent garden, a shrubbery; and Jones assured me that very good judges considered that he had, by judicious planting, imparted to his acre of lawn quite a parkish character.

His daughter, a grave, handsome woman of about thirty, presided over his household, and the dinner did great credit to her management and taste. In the evening, when Miss Jones retired, her father and I drank a considerable quantity of excellent port wine—so much, indeed, that I regret I cannot now recollect, as accurately as I could desire, the very interesting conversation which we then had together. I will, however, attempt to record an outline of it as a suitable preface to the sketch which I am about to write.

Jones assured me that neither his daughter nor any of his Putney neighbours had the slightest suspicion of the real nature of his employment in town. To them he was simply 'a gent in business in the city;' they only knew that he kept a good house, paid his bills with exactitude, was hospitable to his friends, charitable to the poor, and the best churchwarden the rector had ever appointed.

As he became excited by his subject and the second bottle, he attempted to convince me that his avocation was one on which the world frowns with unfair severity. He admitted the evil tendencies of it, but contended that it was no worse than that of the more opulent money-mongers, who, on the eastern side of Temple Bar, avail themselves of the necessities, weaknesses, and vices of their fellow-men, to extort exorbitant profits and usurious interest; and that it was very possible that in the eye of Heaven he might stand no lower than many of the merchant princes of England, who, from their gilded palaces in the West, think themselves entitled to look down with self-satisfied scorn on the low hell-keeper, and like the Pharisee of old, to 'thank their God that they are not as that man is.'

I had a very bad headache the day after I dined at Zero Lodge. I was angry with Jones for having made me tipsy; yet, on thinking over his sophistical vein of reasoning, I could not but see that it was very possible that a good many of our merchant princes, who have their dingy counting-houses in the City, and their town-houses in the far West, and their country-seats all over England, and who hitch themselves on to the peerage by marrying their sons to Irish peers' daughters, and their pretty daughters to stale lords upon town, might, if the truth could be ascertained, turn out to have realised their noble fortunes by practices not much more creditable or useful than those pursued by my friend Jones, although the world, that cringing cur, is too happy to bow down before them in their high places, whilst it snarls and snaps at minor social malefactors like poor Jones, and bites them whenever it can do so with impunity.

My father, having probably heard from some of his correspondents that I had not, during my sojourn in the Temple, adopted that line of life which was most likely to lead me to eminence in the legal profession, wisely thought that the best thing he could do for me would be to remove me from my present associates, and the scene of my follies. He therefore managed to procure for me a diplomatic appointment in South America, where, for several years, I resided as unpaid *attaché* to Her Britannic Majesty's legation at Bogotà.

I was suddenly summoned home to meet my father, whose health had compelled him to leave

Ceylon. We did not, however, meet one another. He died at the Cape, and the vessel in which I had expected him to arrive, brought me the news of his death, and of the fact that I had inherited a fortune of 80,000*l*., the fruits of his laborious and well-spent life.

Although I had never seen my father since I was a child, I was deeply moved at his loss. His letters to me had been rather those of a kind and considerate friend, than of a parent justly irritated at his son's misconduct. I had no other near relatives alive,—and whilst everybody was congratulating me on my newly-acquired wealth, I could not help feeling bitterly that, although as well off as most people for pleasant acquaintances, I stood nearly alone in the world, without a single being who really cared for me.

I had acquired sufficient experience during my residence in South America to make me disinclined to renew the sort of life I had formerly led in London; besides, the crew of the Beauséant were scattered over the face of the globe,—and have, I am happy to say, nearly all turned out much more creditably than might have been prognosticated, when I broke off my connection with them, and sailed for Bogotà. Little Bob Vane, who pulled bow to my stroke, has just got a regiment for his conspicuous gallantry in Scinde, having exchanged his wig for a light dragoon shako soon after I entered upon my diplomatic career; and mad Willy Coote, who steered us the year we licked the Leander so infernally, and who took orders the week after our match, is at the present moment one of the youngest bishops ever raised to the episcopal bench.

I mention these two circumstances that my readers may not entertain too vile an opinion of me, and refuse to read a tale written by the avowed associate of the keeper of a gambling house. Of course, I see but little now of the Bishop of Romford; but I am proud to say, that both he and Colonel Vane retain for me the same esteem which I implanted in their bosoms the day my winning stroke brought the old Beauséant, amidst the shouts of assembled thousands, through the centre arch of Putney bridge twenty boats' lengths a-head of the hitherto unconquered Leander.

My deliberations as to my future moves in the

game of life were cut short by a very commonplace event. I fell in love. In due course of time I married a girl nearly as friendless as myself, and, having no particular local ties, we chanced to settle down in the pleasant county of Herts.

Here we lived for several years, in that passive state of enjoyment, which I believe to be the great desideratum in this vale of sorrows.

My wife—who was, when I married her, a gay, thoughtless girl—became, after presenting me with sundry little Evelyns, a comely, staid, anxious matron; and I liked her all the better for the change. Our children, sturdy boys and pretty girls, grew up around us healthy and well-disposed. Our income was adequate to our wants and wishes; and, whilst I planted, preserved, shot, and enacted magistrate, Mrs. Evelyn gardened, attended to the wants of the poor, and prided herself on her village school. We fancied we did a great deal of good, and I verily believe we did some. The poor, as well as the rich, spoke well of us; we basked in the sunshine of life, and little expected the squall which was about to dismast us,—and that, too, from the brightest quarter of our social horizon.

We lived in a beautiful cottage near Welwyn, which had belonged to the Cowper family, who have large possessions in that part of Hertfordshire. Our neighbours were partly the hereditary lords of the soil, and partly new-comers connected with London, who availed themselves of the vicinity of our shire to town, to run down to their country-houses and ruralise, whenever the cares of state or business would permit.

Hatfield, Gorhambury, the Hoo, and Pansanger, gave us balls during the winter, and were ever ready to promote our gaieties without overwhelming us with condescension or grandeur; and the wealthy Londoners who occasionally took up their abode amongst us, constantly brought down with them some agreeable society, which infused new life and information into our circles.

I believe I may assert, without vanity, that my wife and I were popular people in the county. We liked almost everybody, and almost everybody liked us.

But there was one family in our immediate neighbourhood to whom we were more especially bound by the ties of love, esteem, and admiration.

Jacob Omnium was a leading partner in the great City house of Omnium, Dibs, and Rhino. He was understood to be immensely rich, a liberal in parliament, well with the government, and, in our eyes—which, we flattered ourselves, were pretty sharp ones—was possessed of every virtue under the sun.

He was more than an opulent and successful man of business; he was a philanthropist in the most extended sense of the word. Distressed foreigners clung to him as their mainstay. He was a director, and an active director, too, of every hospital, every asylum, every penitentiary that ever was heard of. At every public meeting for the amelioration of the animal, mineral, or vegetable world, his voice was sure to be heard; and Omnium spoke well. Not content with contributing to the advancement of every praiseworthy institution from his wealthy purse, he made a point of supporting it by the sacrifice of what, to him, was far more important,—his time, and the weight of his name.

In the country he was indeed a valuable neighbour. His habits of business rendered him omnipotent at all county meetings; he prided himself on seeing through people in a moment, and on being as inexorable towards insincerity and imposture, as he was accessible and merciful to frankness and repentance.

I used to be a good deal at his house, which was constantly filled by his ministerial friends from town, who appeared to appreciate equally his shooting, his cellar, his cook, and his conversation. He brought thither also many distinguished foreigners, with whom my knowledge of modern languages made me a favourite. My wife, who sang well and readily, was much courted by Mrs. Omnium, a handsome, good-humoured, fashionable woman; and my boys, although a couple of years younger than Lennox, Omnium's boy, rode and played cricket just as well as the said Etonian anti-climax.

I had, for some time, been meditating on the best scheme of education for my eldest son, John Evelyn. Mary, who had heard great things of Eton from the Omniums, was very anxious I should send him thither; and, indeed, I was much inclined to do so myself, but was deterred by the expense of the thing, for Johnny was the first of a series of five, and my dear wife admitted, with a sigh, that she saw no good reason why the series should not, in due time, be extended to ten.

At last we determined to consult Jacob Omnium. We knew that he was a good and wise man, well acquainted with our position, and we therefore agreed to abide by his advice.

A day or two afterwards I received the following note:—

'Dear Evelyn,—Rufus Redtape is coming here to-morrow with Ckrnfsky for a few days' shooting. I think you would like to meet one another, so pray drive over to breakfast, and bring your gun. Mrs. Omnium hopes Mrs. Evelyn will come to dinner. Ckrnfsky, who is a first-rate musician, is dying to hear her sing.

'Yours, very faithfully,
'JACOB OMNIUM.

'Coombe Abbey, Monday.'

Now, the Hon. Rufus Redtape was under-secretary for foreign affairs, so I was, of course, highly flattered at being selected by Omnium to meet him. Ckrnfsky, too, was a celebrity in his way. My wife wished, above all things, to see him, for she had read a pamphlet published by the illustrious Pole himself, and lent to her by Mrs. Omnium, in which he gave a harrowing account of the wrongs inflicted on him by the monster Nicholas, who had crowned a lengthened persecution by forcibly separating him from his lovely wife, and marrying her to an immense drum-major in the imperial guard, to whom his wretched Katinka had since borne seven children entirely against her will. She had never had any by the Count, which made the injury still more poignant.

As I wish my readers to have as good an opportunity as I can afford them of judging of the eminent virtues of Jacob Omnium, I will, at the risk of being tedious, carefully recount every circumstance which occurred on the occasion of this visit of ours to Coombe Abbey.

It was a fine old monastic building, which Omnium had purchased from a decayed Hertfordshire family, and had embellished at great expense. The house had been restored in the Grecian style, and the park, which had been denuded of its old timber by the necessities of its former owners, was now covered by thriving young plantations, created by the taste of Loudon and the wealth of Omnium.

Everything about Coombe looked as flourishing and prosperous as could be—too flourishing, too prosperous, if possible. It was obviously the residence of a capitalist. Every lodge, farm-building, and cottage seemed as if it had not been erected more than a week. In every corner were stuck freshly-painted boards, warning trespassers to 'beware;' the woods swarmed with game and game-keepers in new shiny plush jackets; there were acres of glass in the gardens, and Grafton, the gardener (quite a scientific man), invariably carried off the biggest gold medal at the Chiswick flower-shows. Omnium's Scotch steward was fatting a huge ox, which the best judges considered safe to win the first prize at Smithfield, if the brute were not smothered in its own grease before that event came off; seven-year-old sheep browsed apoplectically in the park; Omnium's pigs were curious; Mrs. Omnium's dairy and poultry-yard were unrivalled in the county; their horses, both for agriculture and pleasure, were the handsomest and sleekest that money could procure; and as for their dogs, the place was a perfect canine dépôt.

On reaching Coombe, I sent my dog-cart to the stables and entered the front hall just as the breakfast-bell rang. I there found assembled, Omnium, his wife, his children, thirteen maid-servants—all dressed alike and mostly good-looking, seven men in livery, the Honourable Rufus Redtape, and Count Christian Ckrnfsky.

Omnium was too much wrapped up in his devotions to notice my entrance, so I quickly deposited my gun in a corner, and, at a signal from him, we all flapped down on our knees and said the Lord's Prayer, as loud and as fast as we could. He afterwards read two or three very beautiful thanksgivings with great unction, and concluded with the lessons for the day. The thirteen maid-servants then dropped thirteen curtsies, and vanished, abducting the younger branches of the family; but not till Jacob had kissed and blessed them (the branches) with affecting solemnity. The seven men in livery hustled out after the maids, and then Omnium, becoming conscious of my presence, came forward, shook me cordially by the hand, and presented me to Redtape and the Count.

On entering the breakfast-room we discovered a capital hot meal prepared for us by Omnium's man cook (who, being a Frenchman, was not expected to attend family worship) and served up by two staid gentlemen in black, who, from the gravity of their demeanour, might fairly be trusted to work out their salvation in private.

Never was there a man who could jump from grave to gay with such surprising activity as Jacob Omnium. During breakfast he was full of his fun, told us stories which I was very glad my wife was not there to hear, and which even the fashionable Mrs. Omnium declared were too bad, and quizzed Rufus Redtape unmercifully about a foreign countess with a colossal bouquet with whom he had contrived to scrape acquaintance, owing to a crush of carriages at the Opera on the previous Saturday.

The Count and Mrs. Omnium appeared to get on together capitally, although to this day it remains a mystery to me how they managed to interchange ideas; for the distinguished Pole spoke no known language under the sun. He was a small stiff carroty man, with a big head, and bristling moustachios, growing, as it were, upside down, and his conversation, conducted in a sort of Polish-German-French *patois*, seemed, as far as I could make it out, to consist mainly of a series of abortive compliments on Mrs. Omnium's beauty, in most of which he broke down midway from a sheer lack of words wherewith to express his sentiments.

He ate voraciously, chiefly with his knife, which he held like a spoon. His fork he appeared to consider entirely in the light of a toothpick. Yet both my wife and Mrs. Omnium persist to the present day in maintaining that Count Christian Ckrnfsky is the highest bred and most charming person of their acquaintance.

Breakfast being ended, Mrs. Omnium and Ckrnfsky retired to the library (for the little Count had shot so many fellow-creatures in duels and on the battle-field, that he found no excitement in shooting mere partridges), Rufus Redtape and I smoked our cigars under the portico, and our host gave audience to a lot of poor devils who were waiting to speak to him on the lawn. What he said to them I know not, for he piqued himself on doing good in private; but he evidently sent them away rejoicing.

The keepers then brought round the dogs, we shouldered our guns, and forthwith plunged into turnips. A man can't well display his moral excellence whilst partridge-shooting; but still, during the day, we had several occasions for admiring the soundness of Omnium's heart. He was inconveniently particular in ascertaining that every head of game was thoroughly dead before it was bagged; he reprimanded Wad the keeper with almost unnecessary severity for having omitted to apprise Mrs. Omnium that Mrs. Wad had got a milk fever; and our luncheon was sent out to meet us in a five-acre field, apportioned by him to the poor of the parish on a new principle of his own invention.

At dinner Omnium's sallies of wit and moral dicta alternately convulsed us with laughter and filled our eyes with tears. His conversation was chiefly calculated to inspire us with vaguely wide notions of the liberal and extensive commercial operations in which he was engaged.

No man could accuse Omnium of being ashamed of his calling. He gloried in it. He told us, with honest pride, that his head clerk, a most worthy man, had a salary of 3,000*l.* a-year, and a house in Eaton Square; how it was the custom of the firm of Omnium, Dibs, and Rhino to secure a pension of at least a hundred pounds a-year to the family of every individual who died in their service; how he had just got a cadetship from Sir John Hobhouse for his butler's nephew, a very gentlemanlike lad; and how, to oblige his very old friend the Chancellor of the Exchequer, he had made his grandson a supernumerary clerk in their establishment in the Polynesian group.

Never was there such a magnificent and philanthropic merchant prince as Jacob Omnium, by his own account. Yet somehow, whilst he led you to this conclusion, he appeared to be abusing and depreciating himself all the while. In the evening my wife and Mrs. Omnium sang, and the illustrious Pole favoured us with a sort of husky howling, which the ladies told me was a Polish lament; and which undoubtedly was the most lamentable attempt at harmony it has ever been my ill-fortune to undergo.

Both Mary and I felt out of spirits as we drove home. I hope and trust that we did not feel envious of the Omniums; but certainly, if we did not envy them for being so much better than ourselves, we were dissatisfied with ourselves for being so much inferior to them in moral excellence.

The next time I saw Omnium I spoke seriously to him on the subject of Eton. He praised the school highly, averred that it made boys gentlemanlike, and fitted them for mixing in good society afterwards, and assured me, that if I decided on sending Johnny thither, Lennox Omnium and his friend Lord Ptarmigan should look after him for me.

Omnium was essentially a delicate-minded man. He never touched on the subject of expense till I alluded to it myself; and, although he was much too shrewd not to know within a few pounds what my income was, he listened to the details which I gave him with as much interest as if he had then learned them for the first time.

I proceeded to state to him that I should not feel justified in assigning three hundred pounds a-year to the education of my son, unless he could point out to me some way by which I could legitimately increase my income, which was then entirely derived from property in our own funds.

Omnium squeezed my hand affectionately, and said, 'My dear Evelyn, I am a man of business; you are not. It is absurd that your son should be deprived of the advantages of an Eton education, because you lazily choose to let your capital lie fallow in the three per cents. I will consult with Dodger—our chief clerk, a very worthy man—to-day, and will let you know what we decide upon for you when we return from town.'

When Omnium did return from town, he and Dodger had re-arranged my property for me. None of it was to pay me less than seven per cent., whilst the securities on which it was lent, were, in their experienced eyes, far safer than our own funds.

I was to hold the bonds of a young, vigorous,

unencumbered nation, fruitful in resources hitherto undrawn upon, and of republican integrity, in lieu of those of a people groaning under oppressive taxes, an extravagant and heartless aristocracy, and an overwhelming debt. My income was thus to be doubled by this simple financial operation of the great and good Omnium.

He concluded our conference by saying, 'Mind, Evelyn, I do not advise you to do this, for I make it a rule never to give advice on such matters. But I will confide to you that I hold myself 280,000*l.* in the securities which Dodger has suggested to you, and if you decide on investing the whole, or any part, of your capital in the way he proposes, he shall manage the matter for you; as you are not, I know, in the habit of transacting such business for yourself.'

My wife was in raptures when she heard I had adopted Omnium's suggestions. I confess I was in my heart silly enough to be glad that Jacob, notwithstanding the capital stories he told after dinner, was notoriously a man of the most rigid morals, and that Mrs. Evelyn was by no means so good-looking as when I first married her; for Omnium's talents and kindness appeared to have engendered in her mind a sort of monomania in his favour. He was a very handsome fellow, too, not much above forty.

Well, Johnny went to Eton, was placed high for his years, and was very happy there. I cannot say that he derived any very great benefit from the patronage either of the Marquis of Ptarmigan or of Lennox Omnium ; the latter of whom, he informed us by letter, was considered in Eton parlance, 'a horrid suck,' but he did well enough, though he appalled his poor mother when he came home for the holidays, by declining all further commerce with the said Lennox, and announcing his stern determination to fight him next half; a proceeding from which we enjoined him, on pain of our severest displeasure, to abstain.

The Omniums were absent from Coombe all the summer ; but when we were in town for a couple of months during the season they were particularly civil to us, and got my wife invited to several very smart balls. As a small return for their kindness—a very small one, I admit—I withdrew my account from my father's old bankers, Messrs. Rowdy and

Co., and transferred it to the firm of Omnium, Dibs, and Rhino.

Omnium actually condescended to thank me for this mark of confidence in him.

During a trip which he made to the continent with his family, I noticed with concern that the *Times* began to denounce American securities as unsafe. My faith, however, in the merchant prince was firm. I felt convinced that his vigilant friendship would apprise me if anything went wrong, and holding such a stake as he did in the I. O. U. States Stocks, he would, of course, command the earliest and most accurate intelligence on the subject,—far better than that afforded by the mercenary correspondent of a public newspaper.

At last, one morning I read in the *Times*, to my utter dismay, that the Great Western had arrived with the startling information that the I. O. U. House of Assembly had passed an unanimous and solemn resolution, that they preferred going to war with all the world rather than paying their debts; and that their Speaker, the Hon. Washington Chowser, had officially signified this resolution in a printed circular addressed to the holders of I. O. U. bonds.

There could be no mistake about this. The information was conclusive.

I will not attempt to describe my feelings. Every man having a wife and family whom he loves, may imagine, if he can, what his feelings would be if he unexpectedly found a letter on his breakfast-table apprising him that he and his were beggars.

Notwithstanding my own heavy grief, I could not help being sorry for the good Jacob, too. 280,000*l.* is no joke to any man, however rich he may chance to be.

Omnium returned to England in a few days; and when I saw him he was all kindness, never alluded to his own losses, insisted on my stopping to dine with him and Mrs. Omnium just as I was— in my frock-coat and dirty boots—and consoled me with the hope of the State of I. O. U. becoming so inordinately rich that it would be forced to pay its debts, as a man bleeds at the nose, from sheer repletion; a result not absolutely impossible, considering the one-sided nature of their monetary operations.

In the meantime, the noble fellow did not humiliate me by any offer of pecuniary assistance, but he declared that he meant to take me by the hand, and to introduce me to Melbourne, and to say, ' Melbourne, John Evelyn is in distress ; he is my friend. I have been of some service to the government, and have never asked a favour of you yet. I now make a point of your doing something for him. He has already spent several years in South America ; is conversant with the routine of diplomatic business, and is ready to go anywhere, so that the climate be good, the work light, and the salary ample.'

'And Melbourne will do this for me,' continued Omnium. ' I know he will, and I would see and get it done at once, only that I am in doubt as to the best means of introducing you to him. If he were in London, I would ask you both to take a chop together here (we have only a kitchen-maid in town) ; but as it is, I think you had better wait till we get him down to Coombe, where he always comes for the first week's pheasant-shooting.'

I am not ashamed to own that hot salt tears coursed one another down my fevered cheeks as Omnium spoke; I could bear misfortune more manfully than I could bear kindness. I returned home; broke the matter to poor Mary, who behaved like an angel; and we at once began to prepare ourselves for leaving our house, and probably the country, for some time.

October came; the first week's pheasant-shooting was over, yet I heard nothing from Omnium. At last I saw by the county paper that he was entertaining a large party at Coombe; and, although I did not read Melbourne's name in the list of his guests, I thought I would walk over and call on him. Rufus Redtape was there, and was very glad to see me, and condoled with me on my losses like a right good fellow, as I have always found him to be. Omnium and his wife were most cordial, and scolded me for not having brought Mrs. Evelyn with me. I excused her on the plea of ill-health; but the fact was, that we no longer kept a carriage, and the distance was too far for her to walk. Besides, I thought that if they had really been so anxious for our society, they might have invited us to come.

Whilst I remained at Coombe I could not contrive to get a word in private with Jacob, he was so much engaged with his other guests. I certainly did fancy, too, that there was an alteration in his manner towards me—a sort of unnatural heartiness, as it were. He drank wine with me *twice* at luncheon, introduced me to all his most distinguished friends, and praised my wife with what I felt to be almost humiliating pertinacity. As I was going away, he placed his hand affectionately on my shoulder, and whispered, 'I congratulate you, my dear fellow. The packet is in to-day, the I. O. U. sixes have risen one-eighth—Washington Chowser is reported to have had another attack of delirium tremens. Better times are in store for us.'

I had much rather that he had told me what Melbourne was going to do for me, than about the swindling speaker of the I. O. U. House of Assembly; for although it was very natural for him, who held 280,000*l*. in those confounded States' stocks, to watch the slightest turn of the market in his favour, it seemed to me, that as far as I was concerned, there was little room for congratulation. Mr. Dodger had bought in for me at 94, and they were now quoted at '15¾—no sales.'

The enormous stake which Omnium held in American securities appeared to make no difference at Coombe. Better times could hardly be in store for him. His horses, oxen, sheep, dogs, gardener, bailiff, butler, and cook, were sleek and plethoric as ever; Grissell and Peto were erecting a new conservatory for Mrs. Omnium, under the superintendence of Mr. Charles Barry, which was to rival the one at Chatsworth; and Omnium confessed to us at luncheon that he had been ass enough to give, the week before, three hundred and fifty pounds to the well-known Mr. Z. for a cab-horse.

The only relative I had in the world was a cousin; and of him I knew but little. He was an odd, ill-favoured, saturnine old fellow, with a most caustic tongue. He lived like a pauper, although he was known to be very rich; and when he came to my house, which was but seldom, I fear that I was not in the habit of being very civil to him.

At this crisis of my affairs he wrote to me. He said he had just heard that I had been swindled out of a considerable sum of money by a house in the City, whom it was not safe to name on account of their wealth, and that he feared I must be in great distress. He therefore enclosed me a cheque on Messrs. Rowdy and Co. for a thousand pounds, and added, that he had directed them to pay me an annuity of six hundred pounds a-year until my affairs came round.

He further said, that if I would accept this without mentioning the matter either to himself or to anybody else, he would defray the expense of Johnny's Eton and Oxford education; and he begged me to inform my wife, that he had been induced to act thus, out of no cousinly affection for me, but entirely from admiration and respect for her character.

My readers, especially if they are men of the world, will probably imagine that I am writing what is not true; but, upon my soul, I am not. My cousin's name is Grimes, and he generally

lives in a cheap lodging in some street near the
Adelphi. He is the ugliest and most discreditable-looking creature that ever was seen; so
much so, that when the I. O. U. States' stocks pay
up, I shall be ready to bet five pounds that not one
of my readers, even now that they know what a
capital fellow Jack Grimes is, would care to be accosted by him under the bay window of White's in
St. James's Street, in presence of the elderly dandies
daily congregated there. Mary did not like him
originally better than I did, but he had at last
quite won her heart by his kindness to her children.
He had taken a great fancy to Johnny especially,
ever since he had heard of his intention of thrashing
Lennox Omnium when he got big enough to do
so.

On this man we are dependent for our daily
bread. We see him but seldom, for I verily believe the excellent creature keeps out of our way in
order to spare us any feelings of humiliation which
his presence might create. He never mentioned
Omnium's name to me but once, and he then vented
his ire after the following fashion.

'D——d rascal, I know very well he did hold

280,000*l.* in those cursed bonds. How much do you think he holds now? Not a sixpence! He bought in at 58, and when he and that scoundrel Dodger had cried them up to 94, he sold his stock to all the old women and fools, yourself included, who trusted him, and sacked the difference.

'Benevolent man—philanthropist—bah! all sham—all acting—a mere trick of his trade to get up a character in order to enable him to ruin you and the hundreds of other poor people whose money he has got hold of. Although I am an old man, I am not without hopes of living to see the rascal smashed by some of the mad speculations in which his vanity and avarice prompt him to engage.'

Omnium is one of the most fashionable fellows in London. He belongs to all the crack clubs, has a special pane of plate glass in White's window, rides remarkable hacks, and gives concerts and balls, at which he would blush to see such a fellow as old Grimes, even in the capacity of a waiter. So I can easily understand how it is that my cousin does not appreciate him as thoroughly as I do.

Certain, however, it is, that since our circumstances have been reduced, we have seen nothing of the Omniums, neither have we ever been invited to Coombe since the Hon. Washington Chowser promulgated the warlike insolvency of the I. O. U. planters.

It is possible that Jacob may not like to ask me there until he can get Melbourne to meet me; but as that statesman must have more leisure time now than he had a few years ago, I should think he might have been easily induced to come and shoot a few pheasants at the Abbey.

Meantime, Jacob Omnium pursues his brilliant career of commercial enterprise and active philanthropy. He has lately acquired increased popularity in the world of fashion by his laudable efforts towards getting up a subscription for the purpose of erecting, in the neighbourhood of St. James, a set of almshouses for the reception of decayed dandies, members of Brookes', Boodle's, the Travellers', Crockford's, and White's; his name figures daily in the *Times* as director of a dozen companies, in any one of which, according to the prospectus, a man may make a rapid fortune without trouble or risk, and I understand that he is a large holder of original shares in the Chinese North Midland Hydro-Electric Railway—at present.

Mary and I live on quietly at our cottage, and look out eagerly for the arrival of the American packets. Our friends and neighbours have redoubled in kindness towards us. The Bishop of Romford has written to tell me that he shall consider Johnny as his especial *protégé*, and Lord ——, Rufus Redtape's father, sent to us last week to say that he was happy to have it in his power to offer me a writership for my second boy.

I must not omit to submit to my readers a letter which we received from Johnny, a few weeks after the American smash :—

'———'s, Eton, Thursday.

' My dearest Papa,—I have, as I promised, been working very hard, and have gained twenty-five places at trials. My tutor gave me such κυδos for what I did, that I thought he would not much mind my getting into a row ; so as soon as the examinations were over, I challenged Lennox Omnium, who is down at the bottom of his remove, and we fought in the playing fields after twelve.

' I have just licked him in thirty-five minutes,

and though I am afraid you and mamma will be very angry with me, I declare it gives me greater pleasure than all the places I took. I am a good deal cut about, but nothing to signify.

'Tell mamma she must scold Cousin Grimes for it, for he came down here the other day, gave me and some more fellows a dinner at the Christopher, and made me show him Lennox Omnium. Then he gave me a 5*l.*-note, and told me not to mind his being bigger than me, for he was certain I could lick him, and so I have.

'I have not time to write any more, for Cousin Grimes will expect to hear all about it too, and my knuckles are very stiff.

'I remain, my dearest Papa,
  'Your affectionate son,
    'JOHNNY.'

When Mary and I read this letter, I do not believe we envied the Omniums a bit; we both agreed that the chiefest sources of happiness in this world are not those which money can procure.

Still, I cannot help wishing that those infernal I. O. U. planters would book up.

August, 1845.

MR. Z., THE HORSE-DEALER.

READER, I am going to look at some horses at the well-known Mr. Z.'s stables. If you will accompany me thither, I think you will be amused and edified.

Here we are. This sprinkling of bright yellow sand on the foot-pavement is an unfailing token of the vicinity of a horse-dealer's yard. The long passage by which we enter his premises is as clean as paint and care can make it, and is paved with wood. On the right hand, the yard is deeply littered with clean fresh straw, curiously plaited at the edges; on the left the wooden pavement is decorated with more of the bright yellow sand.

Opposite to the entrance is the office, with its clear plate-glass windows, polished mahogany desk, and Turkey carpet. Outside it, on a wooden horse, are three or four saddles, fitting every horse and every rider better than any saddle ever fitted them before, and neither too new or too old, but just of that mellow hue which best becomes a two hundred nag.

Above, on pegs, hang as many bridles, with their bright bits and curb-chains, and fresh *cérise* satin fronts.

Not a soul is to be seen stirring about the place. You need not holloa, reader,—neither Mr. Z. or his people are men to be aroused by such a vulgar style of summons. Do as that shining bright plate directs you : 'Pull the Office Bell.'

Its deep tone resounds through the yard. An inner door leading from the dwelling-house into the office opens, and the polite Mr. Z. presents himself. He is a middle-aged man, well-made, and well-dressed ; his costume is scarcely 'sporting,' and if he be not perfectly aristocratic in his bearing, he only betrays himself by a too visible assumption of the genteel.

He listens intelligently to our description of the sort of animal we require, and then, turning to a younger man than himself, who fills the situation which a dealer in any other article would denominate that of a foreman, he directs him to order out 'the Cheshire horse.' Albert, for such is the name by which the 'confidential friend' (who looks more like a smart young county M. P. than a dealer's man) is addressed, gives his orders in a low tone, and forthwith half-a-dozen stablemen, all exactly alike in size, and attired in marvellously long waistcoats and marvellously baggy breeches, hurry to the box where the Cheshire horse resides.

One bears a beautifully pipe-clayed headstall, a second a mane-comb, a third a silk handkerchief to dust the animal's shining coat; in a twinkling he is ready, and bounces out of his box, led.

He is placed against a white wall, with his forehand on rising ground, to improve the appearance of his sloping and sinewy shoulder. Albert, apparently in a fit of absence, takes up a gig-whip, but does not use it. He merely twiddles the lash about quietly in the yellow sand, and looks innocent. The Cheshire horse, nevertheless, shows the white of his eyes, and evidently views Albert's proceedings with suspicion.

Mr. Z., after permitting us to examine the animal for a short time in silence, exclaims in a solemn tone, 'Let him walk; give him his head.'

Down the deeply-littered ride the noble animal strides, lifting his legs high to extricate them from the fresh prickly straw, and nodding his head at every step. The stableman then attempts to make him trot; but he commences such a series of kicks and plunges, that Mr. Z. stops the exhibition, and proposes that we should see him ridden.

He is saddled in about thirty seconds by the six strappers.

'Get on him, Albert.'

Albert deposes his gig-whip, and mounts deliberately, making the horse remain quiet for a minute after he is settled in his seat. He then, leaving the reins loose on his neck, allows him to walk down the ride once more. His ears are laid back, his muzzle is poked forward nearly to the ground, he bites snakily on either side as he slings down the yard.

'Playful creature!' minces Mr. Z. 'Trot, Albert!'

Albert obeys, and collects his reins. The Cheshire horse acquits himself equally well in this pace. Mr. Z., when his friend is at the further end of the yard, observes privily to you and me, reader, that he wishes one of us would have the goodness to get up and do the horse justice; for that Albert, although an agreeable companion, and much attached to him, is a sad muff on horseback. Yet, to a casual observer, his seat appears firm and elegant, and his hand as light as a lady's.

'Now, Albert, be kind enough to let us see him gallop.'

The ride is rather limited for the purpose; but, on being touched by the spur, the Cheshire horse bounds off like a deer at a pace which must inevitably carry him smack through the office window. Albert can't possibly pull him up in time. Yet he just does manage to do so. The animal comes round with a struggle and a scramble which raises a cloud of straws, and darts to the other end of the yard with increased animation.

You, reader, being a timid equestrian, hint your fears to Mr. Z. that the beast is a little *too* spirited.

'Canter, Albert!' shouts Mr. Z.

In what manner Albert contrives to oil the waves of the Cheshire horse's ardour, I cannot say; but at Mr. Z.'s behest, the reins are dropped on his neck, and he spontaneously subsides into a titupping amble of six miles an hour, which the most dyspeptic invalid might enjoy with advantage to his digestion. On reaching the spot where we stand, he stops stock-still, and, stretching his forelegs well out before him, begins to nuzzle Mr. Z., saying, as plainly as a horse can speak, 'Now ain't I a nice creature?'

Mr. Z., seeing that the horse can speak so eloquently for himself, has too much tact to chaunt him; he therefore leaves you and me, reader, to confer together, and observes in a tone of affectionate reproach to Albert, who sneezes, that he 'told him he would catch cold yesterday, when he *would* swim the Thames with "the Queen's," just because Tom King did.'

'Take in the Cheshire horse and bring out "the Disowned."'

The Disowned is not so showy a horse as the first one—his points are more prominent, his legs are less fresh, he is blemished; in short, he appears somewhat of a screw.

'Do me the favour, sir, to examine that animal with attention—I should like to have your candid opinion of him.'

'He is a fine-shaped, powerful horse, Mr. Z. Is not his off-knee marked?'

'They are both very badly broken, sir.'

'He has also been severely fired for curbs, I see.'

'Very severely indeed, sir.'

'I don't much like his forefeet; they seem weak and flat.'

'He is usually lame on them, sir. That horse, sir, is not for sale, I merely show him to you as a curiosity. He was poor Sir Shovealong Cramwell's famous hunter. We bought him at the late baronet's sale last week. He is a public horse, sir; it is well known that he fetched at the hammer four hundred and eighty-five guineas. When I say he is not for sale, I must explain myself. If any gentleman likes to come forward handsomely, of course he must have the Disowned, but I am not anxious to part with him. Indeed, Percy, my eldest boy, has teased me into a sort of promise to keep him to ride with our beagles. I see you think him a dear horse, sir, but he is only nine years old, and he can come out once a-week, and go clear away from everybody—a child may ride him—he will face anything, and I defy anyone to put him down. I pledge my reputation, that his breaking poor Sir Shovealong's neck was the merest accident in the world.

'Now, take in the Disowned, and bring out "the cob."'

Out bustles a low, thick horse, bay, with black legs, small head, good mane and tail, quick, flippant action.

'This cob, sir, can carry any weight that ought to be carried, and can trot a mile in three minutes. You may ride him with the rein on his neck—he is quite a confidential animal, sir.'

'His price, Mr. Z.?'

'Sir, he is expensive. Albert bought him of

the Bishop of Romford. We *gave* two hundred for him, and had great difficulty in tempting his lordship even at that price. Indeed, I don't think he would have consented to sell him at all, had he not been annoyed at the constant chaffing of the owner of Confidence, the American trotter, who wished to force the bishop, through " Bell's Life," to make a match to trot ten miles in harness.'

'Mr. Z., you have not yet shown me the description of horse I enquired for.'

'I am aware of that, sir ; I *have* precisely the animal you seek, but he is at Z. farm. If you can spare me an hour to-morrow, and will ride down thither, I flatter myself I shall be able to suit you. I merely wished you to examine these horses, because I am confident I shall never have an opportunity of exhibiting three such perfect creatures again.'

'Good morning, Mr. Z.'

'Good morning, sir ; much obliged to you for your kindness.'

Another day, reader, we will go down to the farm together, and see if we can find a nag to suit us.

Mr. Z. is such a civil, good-natured fellow that I should like to deal with him; but when he talks to me of 'public horses' and 'expensive creatures,' I cannot help fancying that he takes me for a fool.

Perhaps he may be right—I must not be a judge in my own case—you, reader, must decide.

March, 1843.

Z. FARM.

READER, I promised you, the other day, that I would let you know when I intended to pay Mr. Z. a visit at his farm. We will, if you please, go down thither to-day.

A ride of an hour takes us into a fine undulating grass country; this old-fashioned, high-roofed, red-brick house, with the large farm-buildings attached to it, is the residence of Mr. Z.

There he is on the lawn before the door, attired in a spicy cut-away, playing with a charming little child—not a little over-dressed, to be sure—but, in these days, Mrs. Z. is not the only lady who seems to aim at making her children look like young *saltim-banques*.

On seeing us, Mr. Z. hands his boy over to the care of a large, rough deer-hound, and comes forward to greet us, calling to his men to take charge of our horses. Albert is also at hand, Mr. Z. says to him:—

'Albert, here is Mr. H. come to try Rococo. Let the Wave, Oliver Twist, and Scroggins be saddled, and tell Percy we shall want him. Meantime, gentlemen, perhaps you will like to walk through my stables.'

Mr. Z. is decidedly intended by nature to be an eminent man in his line. Whatever he attempts to do, he appears to do well. Had he taken orders, he would inevitably have been a bishop—had he gone to the bar, he would have had a very good chance of the woolsack—as it is, he is *facile princeps* amongst his fellow horse-dealers.

Whilst we stroll across the lawn to the stables, I observe that he possesses not only a strong zoological taste, but a good one. That large Scotch hound rolling over and over on the grass so good-naturedly with Master Dudley Z., is visibly *pur sang*, and I would back those perky little terriers which follow us about scratching and sniffing at every cranny susceptible of a mouse, to worry a red-hot poker, if Mr. Z., to whom they seem much attached, were so unreasonable as to put their pluck to such a fiery ordeal.

In one corner of the yard is a row of rabbit-hutches; in another is chained a fine large tame fox. A flight of rare pigeons, too, are to be seen wheeling in circles around the tall chimneys of the dwelling-house.

The stables are not very smart on the outside. They are chiefly divided into boxes. The interior of each box is arranged in a manner calculated to delight anybody who has an eye for the Becoming. There is nothing fine or tawdry, order and good taste are evinced throughout.

Not a horse in the establishment is without some anecdote, very well told by Mr. Z., connected with it: they all appear, according to him, to have been purchased under peculiar circumstances, without which nothing short of the ruin, death, or mutilation of their former proprietors would have induced them to part with such perfect animals. The failure of what are pleasantly termed 'American securities,' the tariff, and the Income-tax, also account for the appearance of a good many in the market.

Mr. Z. states readily the price he has given for

each, and corroborates his assertions by his receipt-book, and by letters from his correspondents in the country, worded thus:—

'Market Harborough.

'Dear Z.,—After a good deal of chaff, I have gammoned Lady K. out of her ponies. I was obliged to give her own price—she knew you meant having them, and said she would be d——d if she bated a farthing. You will agree with me that they are cheap at 180*l.*

'Yours, JOSEPH SNAFFLE.'

Or thus:—

'Mr. Z.,—Scroggins is yours at 250*l.* No other man in England should have had him under double the money. But I am off in rather a hurry for Brussels, and want the ready. You can send it through Lawyer F. by a cheque *crossed* to my bankers.

'SWISHTAIL.'

Such epistles as these save a world of time and trouble. After reading them we either buy Lady K.'s ponies, or Lord Swishtail's steeple-chaser, or we do not; but if we do, there is no loophole left for bargaining, we cannot grudge Mr. Z. fifty or sixty guineas' profit on each transaction.

Mr. Z. appears to have congregated in his stables the *élite* of the equine world. There is a park-hack neater than Lord Gardner's chestnut; there is a lady's horse more beautiful and gentle than Massy Stanley's roan (Mr. Z. remarks on pointing it out, that it would suit her Majesty, but that with her present Civil List she can't stand the price); there is a cab-horse that can step up and go away in better style than D'Orsay's ever-to-be-remembered brown; there are weight-carriers with muscular names, Behemoth and Leviathan, to whom Sober Robin was but a slow weed; there is a trotter, the Bermondsey Pippin, whose speed no man can guess at, it never having been tried; there are hunters for men of ten stone, twelve stone, and fourteen stone, that nobody can either catch, stop, or pound; there are black chargers with small heads and long tails for the Houschold Brigade, confidential cobs for pot-bellied octogenarians, cocktails for M. P.'s who are obliged to support provincial races, steeple-chasers for lads from college, who think it a fast thing to have a nag in 'the Grand National.' Here are no young raw brutes to break customers' necks, they have one and all been tried, and approved themselves worthy of a place in Mr. Z.'s collection.

'The horses are ready, gentlemen; will you have the kindness to mount.'

I get on Rococo; you, reader, whom I have ascertained during our ride down, to be a bit of a tailor, had better stick to your cob and look at us. Mr. Z. backs the Wave, and Percy Z., a boy about twelve, clad in a blouse, no breeches of any kind, with a pair of jack-boots on his naked legs, and without a hat, is tossed upon Scroggins, a blood-like raking steeple-chaser, seventeen hands high, light chestnut with white legs, and evidently a hot one. Albert rides Oliver Twist.

'Now, Percy, where shall we take these gentlemen?'

Mr. Z. is bent on a lark, and I, feeling intuitively that I am on a good one, am not entirely averse thereto, although a married man with a small family.

Percy, Mr. Z., and Albert lay their heads

together, 'the unbreeched one' taking the lead in the consultation, in a remarkable manner, considering his tender age. He is a living proof of the adage :—

> qu'aux âmes bien nées
> La valeur n'attend pas le nombre d'années.

He appears to know to a nicety whose gates are locked, who has, and who has not, yet warned him off their land, and which of the neighbours are still good-natured enough to stand their fences being broken, and their fields galloped over daily by Master Percy and his customers.

We first try the horses over a few wattles in Mr. Z.'s field, but they are too fresh and too near home to jump steadily. We therefore trot away down a lane. Percy and I ride on together. I admire Scroggins' power and strength, but express my suspicion that he must be a difficult horse to hold.

The infant phenomenon affirms with an oath, 'that a child may ride him.'

I enquire, 'Why, if such be the case, he is ridden in a gag snaffle?'

Percy vows it is owing to a mistake of their

people, who are, one and all, 'the stupidest beggars unhung.'

Finally, he proposes that we should exchange horses, and offers me, on his own responsibility, 'to give me Scroggins for nothing, if he does anything.'

This liberal offer I decline, being as yet perfectly satisfied with Rococo.

Having proceeded about a mile, Percy suddenly pulls up, cries to Mr. Z., 'Here we are, father!' rams the spurs into Scroggins, and, turning him half round, tips over a high, new, freshly painted, white five-barred gate, shouting to us to 'come along!'

Albert and Mr. Z. follow him. One crashes through the hedge, the other jumps very cleverly a nasty hog-backed stile. I get into the field, also; but being rather taken by surprise at the suddenness of the evolution, am not at this moment prepared to say how.

You, reader, catch hold of your excited cob's mane, look anxiously over the fence, and suspect me of being in a galloping monomania.

Away we go, led by Percy, straight as a line

across a fine grass country. The horses justify Mr. Z.'s character of them. They are indeed hunters in the fullest sense of the word, resolute yet tractable, they all jump timber, creep doubles, fly ox-fences, and go through dirt and across ridge and furrow as easily and safely as if they were taking a canter on Epsom Downs.

At last, however, we come down on a brook. Scroggins, who is leading, refuses. Mr. Z. and I pull up; Albert gets over with a splash.

The brook is not a wide one, but it is a bumper. The banks are boggy, and it is within a few yards of a goodish hedge and ditch which Scroggins has just jumped, so that he is now on a strip of grass about forty feet wide, the brook before him, and the ditch behind him. He turns restive, and runs back until his hind legs slip into the ditch; Percy flogs and spurs him furiously. Scroggins whisks his tail round viciously, and rears, kicks, and plunges as only a blood horse can rear, kick, and plunge when goaded to desperation. Albert, triumphant at having 'set' Percy, calls to him to mind or he will be hurt. Percy retorts by telling Albert 'to be d——d.'

Mr. Z. looks stoically on. The Father is evidently just now merged in the Dealer.

At last Scroggins begins to exhibit some signs of capitulating; he approaches the edge of the brook; he lowers his head—his forelegs quiver—he seems to be preparing for his spring. 'There he goes!'—Not a bit of it; the brute has jumped deliberately in, and is now attempting to scramble out on the wrong side. The banks are steep, the bottom sticky; it is a matter of uncertainty whether even Scroggins's powers will prevent him from falling back and crushing the brave child, who, nothing daunted, is straining every nerve to extricate himself and his horse.

I, frightened out of my wits at the peril in which the boy is placed, look to Mr. Z., who is as cool as a cucumber, and merely mutters from time to time, as the horse is struggling in the slough:

'You'll be under him, Percy; he'll fall back—no, he won't—well done!—give it him—serve him out—now you're off—no, you ain't—well saved!' and various other similar ejaculations *de circonstance*.

Scroggins, at last, does fall back, but fortunately without injuring Percy, who escapes with a very black mud bath.

After some difficulty we get them both out, and return home, poor Percy sadly crestfallen, and Albert proportionately elated at his rival rider's mishap.

On reaching Z. farm, the horses are led away reeking to their boxes, where a couple of strapping strappers instantly assail each of them with scrapers and wisps of straw.

Mr. Z. invites us in to lunch, and Percy slinks into the house by the back way, to escape the jeers of Albert and the stablemen.

We enter a cheerful room hung round with pictures of celebrated horses, executed by Landseer, Grant, Handcock, and other less distinguished illustrators of the animal world, the gem of the collection being a likeness of Mr. Z. on his renowned steeple-chaser Aëronaut, which he sold for fourteen hundred guineas to carry the Emperor of Russia.

There are also some clever sporting scenes in water-colour, by Alken, and a few sketches by

Mr. Z. himself, who is no contemptible artist in his line.

A book-case at the end of the room contains a well-chosen library of standard works, all good editions.

Mr. Z. does the honours to us with ease and hospitality. The luncheon is plain, but extremely well served; better cleaned plate, better chosen glass and china, whiter table-linen I never saw. The bread and beer are home-made, the butter the produce of his farm, the mutton-chops perfection.

During lunch not a word is uttered relative to business, save that Albert, when he comes in from the stables, mentions, casually, that the Wave (250 guineas' worth) has got a bad cut on the back sinew.

At this unwelcome intelligence Mr. Z. looks rather pleased than otherwise, and respectfully proposes to me a second glass of his excellent brown sherry.

We then adjourn to the garden to smoke a cigar. It is as tasteful and well-kept as the other parts of the establishment. I buy Rococo. Although I am passionately fond of both horses and children, I make it a rule never to expatiate to other people on my own brats and brutes; and I take this opportunity of submitting to my readers, that it would be a great relief if mankind in general would come to the same resolve.

I shall therefore merely state in conclusion, that as the horse chanced to suit me, and as I had pretty good luck with him, having sold him two years afterwards for a hundred more than I gave for him to Lord Tom Towzle, of the Windsor Local Horse, I have no reluctance in proclaiming to the world that I consider Z. to be a pretty fair sort of fellow.

Had the beast pulled an ounce more than I liked, or had I been unable to ride him, or had I had any difficulty in selling him the moment I was tired of him, and had I, when I did sell him, lost fifty pounds by the deal; I doubt whether the English language would have supplied me with sufficiently strong expressions wherewith to stigmatise the villany of the unprincipled Mr. Z.

Poor Mr. Z.!

April, 1843.

THE WILD SPORTS OF MIDDLESEX.

'On Monday, March 1st, Her Majesty's hounds will meet at Salt Hill at eleven.'—*Bell's Life, passim*, March, 1843.

AT half-past nine a string of hack-cabs rolls up to the door of the Great Western Railway station at Paddington. Out of each emerges a gentleman, booted and spurred, attired in a York waterproof, and carrying in his hand a hunting-whip, his only luggage.

One or two horsemen in scarlet ride into the courtyard of the station, and busy themselves in getting their nags 'boxed.'

A few of the Household Brigade, in plain clothes, recognisable by their moustachios, loiter about the place, looking seedy and dirty, as if they had slept out, and had deferred washing and shaving for the day until they reached their barracks at Windsor.

Everybody takes tickets for Slough and buys a newspaper. The bell rings, and one is ushered into a carriage containing eight seats and a remarkably disagreeable close smell.

Seven gentlemen follow, all armed with whips and newspapers. If you are an habitué of the hunt, you probably know most of them by sight, if not personally.

One is Lord——, an ex-ambassador, and a devil to ride; a second is Jack——, suspected of being purveyor of fashionable intelligence to the 'Satirist;' a third, equipped in a hunting cap, is ——, known as chronicler of the deeds of the Queen's Hunt in 'Bell's Life.'

The remainder comprises probably a steeplechase rider or two, and perhaps Mr. Diaper, the swell linendraper, of Ludgate Hill, and young Mr. Omnium, of the great City house of Omnium, Dibs, and Rhino.

During the journey down, the party assembled exchange civilities and morning papers, and discourse of sport, past and to come.

The commercial gents are most loquacious; they appear to know, or to think they know, something about everybody and everything; they aver that 'Rosslyn is a good sort of fellow, but slow;' are decidedly proud of their intimacy with Davis; have a hamper of wine with them as a present to Tom King on his nuptials; and tell infernally long stories corroborative of their acuteness and success in picking up screws for 'a song,' which under their care and management subsequently turn out to be 'trumps.'

The lord doesn't say much, neither is he treated with any very great deference by the Londoners, who don't know that he is a lord; and indeed, it is very excusable that they should have no suspicion of the fact, for he is a singularly gaunt and weather-beaten specimen of his order.

Jack —— and Bell's Life are silent and observant; so am I; and the steeple-chasers swagger and chaff about 'Lottery,' and 'Gaylad,' and the approaching Liverpool.

Whēw, hēw, ēw, w, whiŏu, whiŏu, whēw!

Here we are at Slough. The station is crowded with hunters, hacks, grooms, and bagmen, all awaiting our arrival.

'There's old Rosslyn,' cries young Mr. Omnium,

as the master of the Buckhounds alights from another carriage of our train, and mounts his hack. We follow his example, and ride on together to the meet.

On our way thither, Lord Rosslyn does the civil thing to everybody with great good-humour and effect. A simple 'Good morning, Mr. Diaper; the old horse is looking well,' being sufficient to make the radiant Diaper ready and anxious to take an affidavit belore 'Sir Peter' that Rosslyn is his most intimate friend, and a worthy chap, with no nonsense whatever about him; assertions which elate Mrs. Diaper immensely, and cause her to speculate as to whether Diaper could not invite his friend Rosslyn to dinner; in which case she would secure a man-cook for the day, and get Sir Universal Suffrage, the Radical M.P. for St. Giles's, and the chiefest person of their acquaintance, to meet him.

On reaching the little hillock, well known to all Etonians, opposite Botham's once thriving inn—now, alas! eclipsed by the *Hôtel Monstre* at Slough—we find Davis, Tom King, the second whip, and the hounds.

A good many officers belonging to regiments quartered at Windsor, and a few farmers and counttry gentlemen are with them.

The gents from town talk confidentially to the servants of the Hunt, look out for nods from the country gentlemen, and patronise the farmers immensely.

'Here's the deer!'

A neat claret-coloured van, driven by a man in the Royal livery, passes rapidly by, escorted by 'old Bartlett' on horseback, and by 'Paddy' on foot.

A crowd of pedestrians follow it as well as they can. We, roadsters, trot after the deer-cart, leaving behind us the hounds, and such gentlemen as purpose riding the first burst.

After proceeding a couple of miles north-east of Slough, the van stops in a lane, and is backed against a hedge; the driver climbs on the top, and opens the doors.

There is a brief pause. Then, out bolts a bulky animal with slight limbs and no horns. He clears the fence at a bound, and trots hurriedly to-and-fro in the field adjoining.

The Wild Sports of Middlesex.

A shout from the foot people, who clamber over the fence and run after him, makes him decide on his line, and off he goes at a slinging trot, clearing every obstacle which presents itself to him with ease. He is speedily out of sight.

There being as yet no hounds to ride to, the assembled horsemen look to Paddy, who always knows much better than the deer which way he means to go. Paddy is already a quarter of a mile a-head, pointing towards Uxbridge, surrounded by a hundred men in scarlet, riding before, behind, and very often nearly over him, circumstances which appear nowise to disturb his equanimity, or damp his ardour for the chace.

I and the gents from town wait until Davis and the pack arrive. He trots up the lane, surrounded by the hounds. The instant they espy the deer-cart they give tongue, and scramble over the hedge. Davis follows them very neatly; others try to do the same, less successfully. There is a violent shindy caused by horses jumping, refusing, and falling. One or two are already to be seen running riderless.

The hounds, perplexed by the crowd thus pressing upon them, are at fault for a moment; a clod in a tree holloas, pointing forward to the line. Davis blows his horn and lifts them. They hit off the scent once more, and away they go across the country, heads and sterns down, like a flight of pigeons.

Tom King sticks to them. About five or six other men do likewise. On the left, Dicky Vyse, Beauchamp Proctor, and Billy Baillie of the Blues, lie well alongside the leading hounds. Stout Makepeace follows gallantly in their wake, as well as his weight will permit. On the right, Davis glides smoothly along, whilst Jem Mason and Allan Macdonough are racing with one another, looking out eagerly for big places to jump.

A dozen others follow, or attempt to follow, with but indifferent success; for the scent is good, the country deep, the fences stiff, and the pace 'undeniable.'

The rest of the field disperse in various directions. Bartlett gallops along the road to the right. Lord Rosslyn vanishes down a green lane. The body of the hunt enquire for the best kept and best watered road they can hear of, and stick to it.

Loud is the clatter of horses' feet on the Macadam.

We bang along, best pace, for four or five miles, until we arrive at cross roads. Paddy and his 'tail' are there before us. He is telegraphing from a gate-post, and shouts to his followers as he jumps down, and runs off at a steady dog-trot. 'The deer has his head for Harrow—the road to the right, gentlemen!'

We gather up our reins to follow his advice, when somebody cries out:

'Hold hard; here he is!' and the poor beast rushes through a gap in the hedge, smack into the midst of us.

After a good deal of vociferation and cracking of whips, he resumes his point towards Harrow, and we soon hear the cry of the hounds coming up in pursuit.

Presently we see them racing across a large ploughed field, and Davis, who, as well as the second whip, has anticipated them by some short cut, prepares to stop them.

Dicky Vyse, Proctor, and Baillie are still with them; also Tom King, whose horse is sadly blown.

Baillie's black nag has its head and ears all over mud, having treated its master to a cropper; and Makepeace, who is well in with the others, has lost one of the skirts of his black coat.

The steeple-chasers don't turn up. They have probably succeeded in their obvious object, in breaking their own necks or their horses' hearts, in the shortest possible time.

The whole party have evidently had, what Mr. Diaper is pleased to term 'an enjoyable four-and-thirty minutes.'

Davis and his men contrive with difficulty to stop the pack, which stand baying at him in a semicircle. The crowd increases, and the steam from the horses becomes intolerable. In ten minutes the hounds are laid on again. Davis mounts a fresh horse: the second whip takes up the running from Tom King, who nurses his horse carefully along the road; the Blues, who have not had half enough of it, make sail again, and are joined by a few fresh hands, who have not hitherto 'gone.'

We, Macadamites, get forward along the Queen's highway towards Harrow.

After a time, however, the road and the deer

take different lines; we see the hounds a mile ahead, attended only by a single horseman; the green fields in every direction are studded with red coats.

In a fit of frenzy we deviate into a green lane; becoming still more excited, we open a gate into a field, and adventure upon a cart track; the track ends in a heap of manure; we desperately crawl through a weak place in a fence; and, our blood being up, jump a couple of rotten hurdles; and there we are, entangled in the heart of the Harrow country!

The deer and the hounds may be gone to York for all we know or care; for, on collecting our scattered senses, we find that we have objects of major import to attend to. We are in the enemy's camp, the country far and wide is up in arms against us; no man will tell us the way to the nearest road; insidious clods only pretend to open gates that they may get a grab at our reins as we pass through; others, infuriated, flourish pitchforks in gaps, and accost us in terms *peu flatteurs*.

We bestir ourselves like men to extricate ourselves from this unhandsome fix, and ride as we never rode before, or intend to ride again. Some get falls, and are led away into captivity by the lords of the soil; but the survivors, of whom I have the good fortune to be one, after escapes of a perfectly Affghan character, manage to gain the high road from Uxbridge to London, where they hail the seventh milestone with joy, not, I trust, unmixed with gratitude.

As we trot merrily towards town, we are joined by 'Bell's Life' and the City gents, who, in high spirits at their escape, amuse themselves by a very successful interchange of facetiæ with the 'bus cads and costermongers on the road.

Near the Hippodrome we unexpectedly hear a clamour of dogs—town dogs. A crowd is collecting; policemen are seen in a state of activity; we ride up; a dusty, sweated, jaded beast, which at first sight we take to be a mad jackass, trots wearily along the footway, pursued by a lot of curs snapping at his heels. It is the unfortunate deer once more!

'How devilish lucky!' exclaims 'Bell's Life,' rousing his horse with the spur; 'not a soul up but ourselves;' and onwards we all go towards the Regent's Park.

Several cabs join in the chace—a Hansom's patent having decidedly the best of it.

A man in the Royal livery gallops past us; it is Bartlett, who, having been thrown out, guessed the deer was for town.

A couple of hounds are with him—they take up the scent, and we enter the park, much to the astonishment of everybody—ourselves included.

The deer rushes down the first area he finds open; policeman B. 27 bangs-to the gate, and the day's sport is ended.

Paddy—the ubiquitous Paddy—runs up to assist Bartlett in securing the deer, and I ride home, leaving the commercial gents perfectly frantic with delight, trusting to 'Bell's Life' on the following Sunday for accurate particulars of the run.

Here they are—verbatim—as they appeared in that justly popular print :—

'CLIPPING THING WITH THE QUEEN'S.'

'On Monday last, Her Majesty's hounds met at Salthill. There was a strong muster of cracks of the right sort, amongst whom we noticed the noble Master of the Buckhounds, Lord Tom Towzle, Sirs Shovealong Cramwell and Stumpy Dubs, Captains Roake, Swizzle, Sprogyns, and Snobbe; Messrs. Omnium, Diaper, Smythe, Browne, Whyte, and Greene; and the dashing Mrs. Highflier, on her favourite gelding by Filho.

'The famous deer, Hampden, was enlarged in a field belonging to that fine old English sportsman, Major Flugster (who, we fear, will be unable again to join the hounds this season in consequence of a severe injury to the spine which he experienced last Sunday, after Divine service, in riding a four-year-old over the turnpike-gate on Windsor bridge for a bet of six dozen of bottled ale); and after a short ring of an hour and a quarter, went away straight for Harrow, closely followed by a select few, "wot can do the trick."

'Crossing the grass below the hill, the gallant animal put his nob towards town, and, passing through the villages of Neasden and Willesden, was eventually apprehended by a policeman in the Regent's Park, after a run of three hours and a half, unexampled in severity.

'It was racing throughout, and "no mistake." Only four men saw the thing from end to end, and we have real pleasure in being enabled to point them out to the admiration of their brother sportsmen:—

'Captain Fatman, on Beanstalk; Messrs. Diaper and Dibs; and a hard-riding gent in a hunting cap, connected with the London press, formed the fortunate quartette.

'There were, of course, many falls; and some idea of the superiority of the day's sport may be formed from the fact that two men, a boy, and seven horses have since died from over-exertion and injuries received during the run.

'We regret to add, that it was considered necessary to destroy the gallant Hampden;[1] the hardness of the roads in the vicinity of the metropolis having entirely obliterated the horny portion of his feet.'

---

[1] Is not this a strong argument in favour of wood pavement?— ED. *Bell's Life.*

THE FATHER OF THE FANCY.

SOME few months since, one William Sykes was brought up to Bow Street Police-Office charged by Horsford, the active officer of the Society for the Suppression of Cruelty to Animals, with being the proprietor of an establishment where dog-fights 'came off,' and where badgers were habitually 'drawn,' and cats worried, and rats massacred. He was a rugged veteran, white-haired, bloated, lame and monoptical, and was affectionately addressed by a crowd of sporting-men, who clove to him in his adversity, as 'The Father of the Fancy.'

Mr. Hall, the magistrate on the bench, appeared to have had some previous police-passages with Mr. Sykes, and speedily accommodated him with a month's tour upon Brixton Mill; for the irritated old man recklessly pleaded guilty, exclaiming passionately, that he cared not what became of him; that his trade had been ruined by the unconstitutional interference of the Society, whose agents would not, now a-days, permit noblemen and gentlemen 'to fight a main of cocks, try a pup at a badger, or worry a cat or a few rats over their wine of an evening in peace and quiet.'

He vowed bitterly, that 'he'd as lief rot in quod as bide at home and see the best blood in England a heating the hosflesh of idleness!'

I chanced to be sitting on the magistrate's bench as an amateur 'beak,' when this affecting scene occurred, and was so deeply struck by the poor old fellow's indignant and unaffected grief, that I determined on paying him a friendly visit as soon as he had accomplished his month upon the treadmill.

Accordingly, on Saturday last, I proceeded to Cerberus Cottage—his residence in Kensal New Town—accompanied by my faithful pug, Toby.

I there found the venerable Father of the Fancy and his wife calmly seated in their dining-room, over their post-prandial brandy-and-water;

the latter being lazily employed in the lady-like occupation of trimming the cars of a litter of bull-terrier puppies. The room was enlivened by a first-rate collection of likenesses of the most distinguished canine gladiators of the past and of the present, whose lineage and exploits Mr. Sykes expatiated upon with a degree of interest altogether incomprehensible to me, inasmuch as such a strange family-likeness pervaded all the portraits, that none but a most practised fancier could discriminate between ' the silibrated Ecclesfield Nudger, wot licked the Tooting Trump in ninety-sivin minutes,' and 'the silibrated Whitechapel Nonparel, wot killed Johnny Broom's original fighting-monkey, last Good Friday wos a year.'

They were all white—had one black-eye a-piece—heads like coal-scuttles—powerful shoulders and loins—parenthetical fore-legs—slender sterns—cork-screw tails, and were preternaturally under-jawed.

On our expressing a wish to view his establishment, the Father of the Fancy ushered us into his 'pit,' a large empty room, fitted up all round with benches, and lighted with gas, where Mr. Sykes junior, and his two kids 'wos a-having a bit of diversion with a badger,' being assisted in the operation by a desperate little ruffian of a terrier, well known in 'the drawing circles' as 'the Borough Dentist.'

In the centre of the room was a long narrow box, with a door at one end, containing the badger, who was drawn up on the defensive at the other end; Jimmy Sykes, an undersized child of nine years old, knelt by the side of the apparatus, tenderly sponging away the blood which covered the 'Dentist's' head. Presently his little brother opened the door of the box—in went the 'Dentist' like a shot, yelling with savage ecstasy. A smart scuffle then took place for a few seconds inside; and, then, at a sign from his father, who sate on the edge of the pit, apathetically smoking his pipe, Jimmy lugged the dog out by the tail, whilst the dog lugged out a badger three times as big as himself by the nose.

After much perilous choking, the animals were separated by the children; the badger was replaced in his box by the aid of a pair of tongs, the Dentist's mouth was washed out, the kids took breath, Mr. Sykes junior had a couple of go-downs of brandy-and-water. and then the operation was again and again repeated, until boys, bull-terrier, and badger were utterly exhausted.

The moment poor Toby espied the badger, he set up a dismal howl, and fled with a speed I had not previously attributed to him. I saw him no more till I returned home, when he was discovered in a state of extreme mental and bodily prostration concealed in the coal-hole, from which he was only induced by the pangs of hunger to emerge.

I in vain interceded for the animals, and endeavoured to stop 'the sport.' Mr. Sykes junior and his kids assured me that the Dentist liked it—as, indeed, he most undoubtedly and unaccountably did—and maintained that 'badgers was so tough, that nuffin couldn't hurt them.' So we left the family party to their singular pastime, and proceeded with the 'Father of the Fancy' to the bulldog department, which he considers his especial province, looking down upon 'drawing' and 'ratting' as mere child's play.

In an area of about fifty yards square as many bull-dogs were tethered to posts by short and, fortunately, strong chains; for as I entered the yard they sprang at me with a unanimous and appalling yell. Mr. Sykes raised his hand, reprovingly, and they at once slunk back into their kennels, abashed. He then introduced me to them, assuring me fondly that they were, like many other members of society, the 'good-naturedst' creatures in existence, 'if so be as they warn't haggravated.' And in less than two minutes I found myself patting and fondling indiscriminately a set of the most truculent villains, as far as appearance went, that ever growled under a go-cart; and they on their part, seemed much pleased with the confidence I so blindly reposed in them.

There was Old Crib—the oldest inhabitant of the yard, blind and toothless (his grandfather or great-grandfather, I forget which, had belonged to the Regent); there was Young Crib, sadly masticated about the head in consequence of a recent encounter; there was Mungo and Snob, and Slut and Nettle, and Brat and Grinner, and the Pottery Lass—a brindled bitch as belonged to 'an imminent surgery gent'—and Captain Famish's famous mastiff, as 'ate the cab boy;' and then there were three of the quickest ratters in the world, 'as could be backed for a hundred a-piece to worry against anything of their weight;' and there were scores and scores of devoted rats in wire cages, which the Father handled, unbitten, with marvellous impunity; and, lastly, there was his favourite badger, the 'Stiff-un,' which he informed us, with honest pride, no canine artist, barring his own 'Dentist,' had ever yet been able to draw.

Mr. Sykes admitted to me confidentially, that although the good old English sports of bull-baiting and dog-fighting might be considered to be virtually extinct, he continued to earn a tolerable livelihood by breeding these gallant monsters for the foreign and colonial markets. He said that he didn't want to fight any more public matches—as Parliament didn't wish it—but that he thought it hard 'that a cove mightn't enjoy hisself as he liked in his pit with a few friends.' He asked me why, when Her Majesty's Hounds chevy a poor tame deer along the hard road, till his feet drop off, and then tear him to pieces, the humane public approve of the transaction, and term it 'A clipping thing with the Queen's,' and why, when Prince Albert's beagles more deliberately towler a wretched hare to death, at the rate of six miles an hour, ultimately eating her alive, they congratulate his Royal Highness on having had 'capital sport ;'—the Society's officers, said he, 'don't never meddle with steeple-chasing ; I never heerd tell of their lagging the nobby young dove butchers at the Red House—they darn't say a word to swells as bags their two thousand head of game in three days; but they makes a pint of giving me, and such as me, a month at Brixton, regular, if I only just stands my poor dogs a couple of rats all round, to hanimate 'em, or if they catches me a lending the badger to little Jemmy and his pals to keep them out of mischief on a Sunday afternoon. You knows a thing or two, Mr. H. I wish you'd explain to me this here partial conduct of the Society. How comes it that sauce for the goose ain't sauce for the gander with them?'

As I should have been extremely puzzled to explain why that ancient dictum was inapplicable in the cases thus pertinently put by the Father of

G

the Fancy, I abruptly tendered to him a crown piece, and, simulating great anxiety for the fate of the truant Toby, departed, meditating deeply over what he had said.

ANIMAL MAGNETISM.

I WAS one morning in the act of scolding my servant for his carelessness in having allowed the dog-stealers to get hold of the loveliest little fright of a terrier that ever looked like a tow door-mat on castors, when a friend of mine, an experienced Cockney, happened to call upon me. He was, as usual, followed into my room by an old spaniel bitch, his inseparable companion.

'How do you contrive,' enquired I, turning to him, 'to keep old Bessie out of the clutches of these rascals?'

'Compose yourself, my dear fellow,' said he, 'and I will tell you. Twenty years ago, I came up to town, raw and inexperienced as you are. I was fond of animals, and kept a dog, or rather tried to keep one, to mitigate the dreariness of a bachelor's fire-side. I took pains to procure a handsome beast, but long before he had time

> To know me well
> And love me, he was sure to

be stolen. *Sic de cæteris*, to the number of about half-a-dozen. At last I bought old Bess, then a puppy. She soon followed her predecessors. I, as usual, advertised; paid an exorbitant reward; and, after some trouble, succeeded in recovering her, in order that she might be stolen again the very next week.

'She was of course well fed and well treated in my establishment; yet the fool seemed absolutely to connive at her own abduction, although when in the hands of the dog-stealers she was evidently starved and ill-used. The moment my hall-door was opened, out scampered Bess; and there was invariably some ill-favoured vagabond lurking about the street who instantly captured her, and conveyed her *in ignota loca*. She was never intrinsically worth five shillings, yet I could not help liking her sufficiently to pay away guinea after guinea for her ransom, and it used to pain me sadly to see the evil plight in which the poor beast invariably returned home after a week's detention in the crypts of the Fancy.

'At last, I fortunately bethought me of coming to an amicable arrangement with our persecutors. I directed my servant to permit Bess to be once more stolen. This he very easily contrived for me. I then, as usual, advertised; and as I was by that time well known to be a thorough gentleman, incapable of taking any unfair advantage of the confidence reposed in me by the Fancy, an eminent member of that profession brought Bess to my door one evening, after dark.

'My servant then told him from me, that I should always be perfectly willing to pay a guinea whenever my dog was captured; but that I earnestly entreated him and his friends in future, as soon as they had secured her, to knock at my door at once and claim their guinea, without taking the trouble to carry her home; as, by so doing, they would save their time and my own, spare me the expense of advertising, and her the *désagrément* of fasting in some damp cellar until she was redeemed.

'My servant delivered my message.

'Well,' said I, 'what did the fellow think of the proposal?'

'"Why, sir, Bill Sykes seemed quite unprepared for your kindness. He drawed his hand across his eyes, and said that such conduct was handsome—wery handsome, indeed—and that it would be well for the labouring classes if there were more nobs like you."

'But, does he agree?'

'"Yes, indeed, sir, he does; and he begged me to give you his duty, and to tell you that, if he could prevent it, nobody shouldn't never prig Bess but hisself, and that he hoped he'd have the luck to pick her up again soon, as his wife was in the family-way, and he wanted a trifle to meet the expenses of her confinement."

'Since that time,' continued my friend, 'Mr. Sykes, with my dog under his arm, generally calls for his guinea about once a quarter. Bess has become nearly as fond of him as she is of me, and he certainly has had influence enough over the other members of the confraternity to prevent any of them meddling with his *protégée*. Whenever she is missing, I feel no uneasiness. I merely conclude that Mr. Sykes is about to call for his quarter's salary. Some years ago, on the occasion of Mrs. Sykes being brought to bed of twins, he got me to advance him a couple of pounds, which the industrious fellow honestly worked out in the course of a fortnight.'

Much as I admired my ingenious friend's philocynical treaty with Mr. William Sykes, I was too angry to adopt his arrangement, and proceeded at once to Bow Street, in order to endeavour to recover my dog through the assistance of the police.

The inspector listened attentively to my tale, noted down accurately my description of the animal, and assured me very earnestly that within twenty-four hours every policeman on duty in London should have instructions on the subject.

'But do you think there is any chance of their finding my dog?' I enquired in a piteous tone; for I prided myself on Philibegs, I loved him like a brother, and he cordially reciprocated my affection. Though a perfect little fiend to everybody else, he hardly ever bit me.

The man looked cautiously in my face, as if to

ascertain whether I was laying a trap for him or not, and at last said :

'None in the least, sir; we can do nothing with these dog-fanciers—they are so sly. They would rather kill your dog for the value of his skin, than let you have him again through our interference.'

'What do you advise me to do, then?'

'Why, sir, I am wrong perhaps in telling you, but if you are very anxious to recover the dog, and if you don't care much about punishing the parties as stole him, there *is* a house of call for the Fancy in Lisson Grove; and if you go there and speak civilly to the landlord, he'll be sure to get your dog for you for a very small sum; for these cunning fellows would rather let him go home to you than sell him for double the money to a stranger. If you receive him, they know where to look for him when they want him again.'

The Inspector wrote me down the address, which for obvious reasons I do not publish; it can be had at any police-office; and, through the mediation of the landlord of the public-house— a most respectable man, to whom I paid a guinea in advance — Philibegs was dropped down my area one foggy evening. But he was soon recaptured by the enemy, and I was ultimately obliged to capitulate, and subscribe four guineas annually to Mr. Sykes, on condition that my dog's person should be held sacred by the whole profession. The money is paid quarterly, and nothing can be more honourable than the manner in which Mr. Sykes fulfils his engagement. I have thus the double satisfaction of knowing that Philibegs is secure, and that, as far as I am concerned, Mr. Sykes has been transmuted from a thief into an honest man.

On one occasion, indeed, since this arrangement, Philibegs disappeared for a few hours. I immediately sent for Mr. Sykes, who heard of the terrier's abduction with unfeigned anger and anxiety, and declared that it must have been the act of some tyro in the noble science. He went away assuring me that the animal should be forthwith sent home.

The next day, however, he returned without my dog, and affirmed in the most positive manner that it had not been *stolen*. ' If any of our young men had picked him up,' observed he, 'I'd have been safe to have knowed it.' He expressed his conviction that the animal had either strayed or met with an accident; and sure enough, shortly afterwards Philibegs was led home by the poulterer's boy, whom he had followed as far as Duke Street in hopes of a giblet.

The London Fancy, as the profession proudly term themselves, are a powerful, united, and enlightened corporation. They are called dogfanciers because they are in the habit of indulging practically in strong fancies for dogs which do not, strictly speaking, belong to them. It is a very remarkable circumstance that even the shyest and most savage dogs invariably exhibit the greatest good-will and affection towards every member of the Fancy, although those gentlemen are by no means distinguished from other members of the community either by their personal beauty, or by the superior amenity of their manners.

I have often read of love at first sight; but being a fat man, of an unromantic turn of mind, I never believed in it until I one day saw a fancier operate upon the dog of an old lady who lives opposite to me in Brook Street. It was an Italian greyhound, the most delicate, timid little sylph in the world. It always seemed to be picking its way about the world on the tips of its toenails, and shivered with affright at the very aspect of a strange dog or man.

Whilst I was eating my breakfast I observed an ill-looking fellow sneaking about the corner of the street; but as it was *after* I had become one of Mr. Sykes' *abonnés*, I knew that Phil was in no danger, and merely watched the Fancier's motions from curiosity.

He strolled carelessly backwards and forwards for a few moments. Presently the greyhound slipped up the area steps, crossed the street to him, and deliberately swaggered off at his heels in company with two bull-dogs of singularly disreputable mien and manner. What the man had done thus suddenly to change the lap-dog's nature I cannot divine, hitherto it would not even permit its neighbour Philibegs to give it a friendly sniff, without beginning to yell like a demon; yet there it went swaggering up the street with its tail as stiff as a crowbar, exchanging the most familiar canine civilities with its truculent companions as confidently and unconcernedly as if it had recently licked them both in a fair scratch fight. As the old lady was much attached to her greyhound, the fancier made ten pounds by his morning's work.

I understand that the profession is much followed by the élite of the youth of Whitechapel, Paddington, and the Seven Dials. They cannot afford to hunt or shoot; and the same tastes and motives which lead a member of Crockford's to devote himself to those exciting pursuits impel the fast young butcher and baker of the metropolis to indulge in the passion for the Fancy. It is an occupation which affords opportunity for a display of skill and presence of mind; it is healthy, being carried on in the open air; it brings those who indulge in it into contact with the animals whose society they most like, and there is just sufficient risk in the thing to make it exciting.

Should they get into trouble through their predilection for the sport, the legal penalty which they thereby incur is so slight and salubrious, that it can scarcely be viewed in the light of a punishment. A fortnight on Brixton Mill, in agreeable and improving society, on plain but wholesome prison-diet, just gets a fellow into prime condition, and is, perhaps, the best accident that can occur to a man of pleasure too deeply plunged in the vortex of London society. I learned these particulars from Mr. Sykes, at whose villa at Kensal Green I have since passed many agreeable and instructive hours. He always mentions my friend with gratitude as having been the first philanthropist who attempted to elevate the profession of a dog-stealer, by thus divesting it of all appearance of dishonour, and reducing it to a mere game of skill played between two individuals for a guinea, the object of the one being to retain the animal, and that of his adversary to carry him off.

I think I may as well conclude by informing my readers that Mr. Sykes deals in dogs as well as fancies them. With twenty-four hours' notice he will undertake to supply any number and species of dog, making a reduction of 50 per cent. if they are immediately exported and no questions asked; and if any person should require a tyke ready and able to pin a bull, draw a badger, fight any living thing of its weight—not being particular as to a few pounds one way or the other—or kill cats and rats against time, he cannot do better than apply at Cerberus Cottage, Kensal Green. Mr. Sykes has always a score or two on hand, and is never out of rats. His celebrated fighting monkey, I lament to say, was slain in single combat with the Whitechapel Dentist last Christmas Eve, but he still boasts a badger which no canine artist has yet been able to draw.

His grandson, a very promising kid of ten years old, is always open to scrunch rats with his teeth—his hands being tied behind him—at a pound a dozen, and Mr. Sykes himself can be backed by a sporting marquis, who is to be heard of at Mother Emerson's, for from 50*l.* to 500*l.* to draw any badger in England in a similar manner, barring his own notorious brock—'the Stiff'un.'

THE MAN WHO LIVES FOR HIMSELF.

> Circæis nata forent, an
> Lucrinum ad saxum, Rutupinove edita fundo
> Ostrea, callebat primo deprendere morsu
> Et semel aspecti litus dicebat echini.—*Juvenal.*

SUPPOSING that 'echinus' were the Latin for a Dublin Bay haddock, which my eldest boy, who is at Eton, offers to bet me five to two it is not, the above-quoted passage would apply, even better than it already does, to that middle-aged man, verging on corpulency, who is to be seen every morning in pleasant converse with Mr. Grove, the worthy and well-known fishmonger of Bond Street.

Mr. Stuart Puddicombe is of a florid and cheerful countenance; healthy, yet inactive-looking; neatly, but easily dressed; not a tight string or button about him.

With him digestion is the main object of life;

he despises the possessor of a weak stomach, and envies a ghoul.

Yet he is no gormandiser, he is too far-sighted for that; although he considers it a duty which he owes to himself to obtain, daily, as good victuals as talent and money can procure; yet he so contrives, that the dinner of to-day shall not impair the breakfast of to-morrow; he strictly abstains from a third help of turtle on the Monday, prudently mindful of the haunch to which he is bidden on the Tuesday.

He rises early. With him health is everything; for without health digestion will not go on; and without digestion, appetite is not.

A walk in the Parks prepares him for his breakfast, a light but dainty meal; a little boiled fish, some marmalade, a pat of Bruce's butter, a couple of rounds of crisp toast, and one cup of choice tea from Antrobus—that is all.

The lighter parts of the 'Morning Post,' police reports, fashionable news. murders, and horse advertisements, occupy his mind agreeably till eleven, when he strolls down to Grove's, to ascertain whether the day's supply be good, and also to discover, from the directions pinned on the fish already bespoke, what dinner-parties are about to come off.

At twelve he proceeds to his Club, to collate the police reports of the 'Post,' with those of the 'Herald' and 'Times.' He also takes occasion to learn how the previous day's dinner has agreed with such of his trencher-fellows as he falls in with. He speaks approvingly of A.'s dry champagne, of which, he fears, there can be but little remaining; and joins earnestly in the damnation of B.'s '34 claret, a rough and loaded wine.

He compiles a party to Greenwich for the following Sunday, selecting the component members of it rather from the vigour of their intestines than their wits, cautiously excluding 'poor devils who have no stomachs,' of whom he speaks with contemptuous compassion, and ardently enrolling 'fellows who don't say much, but enjoy their bottle of claret.'

In order to fill up the vacuum in his existence caused by the interval between the publication of the morning and evening papers, he is ready to take a walk with anybody anywhere.

Though he knows and cares nothing about horses or betting, he will willingly accompany you to Tattersall's; or he will as willingly stroll with you into the city, to look at the New Exchange, although he has seen it a dozen times—merely because with him exercise and appetite are cause and effect.

At four, the evening papers recall him to his Club. If not already engaged to dinner, he lays himself out for being picked up by some Amphytrion in good repute. He shakes hands warmly with the owner of the Woodmill salmon he saw in the morning at Grove's; he tells the Dublin Bay haddock a capital story; he whispers a bit of scandal into the ears of the cod's head and shoulders; he affirms that he never before in his life saw the Johnny Dory looking so fresh.

Being a jolly inoffensive fellow, and an A 1. trencherman, he generally succeeds in making one of these fish bite; but if their tables happen to be full, he cheerfully proceeds to order his dinner at his Club, and looks out for a pleasant companion to eat it with him.

This he does carefully and deliberately, not

writing down rashly from the bill of fare those dishes whose names hit his fancy most, but ascertaining surely, by a personal interview with the steward, what soups are freshest, what vegetables least in season.

Wishing to rest his viscera, he stints himself to a pint of sherry and a bottle of light claret, and then betakes himself, half-price, to the play, or knocks the balls about apathetically in the billiard-room for half-an-hour, or indulges in a French novel and a snooze in an arm-chair in the library till midnight, and then to bed.

He belongs to three or four of the best clubs; has a small lodging somewhere; and is to be seen about town all the year round, saving, now and then, a week at Brighton or Paris.

He is not much given to ladies' society; and thinks in his heart that they rather spoil a dinner-party than otherwise. They, on their part, aver that his love of eating is disgusting; yet are mighty civil to him when he dines at their houses; for they fear his influence over their husbands, and know that he is recognised as a just though severe judge in all matters of culinary interest.

He thus lives on agreeably and merrily—if, indeed, his career be not abruptly cut short by apoplexy—till Dyspepsia and Reflection overtake him; and then I decline to trace his career any further, for it is a melancholy one: and in this sublunary scene we stumble over more than sufficient causes of sadness without going out of our way to seek them.

HORSE-BUYERS AND HORSE-SELLERS.

Audi alteram partem.

I DO not believe that on the face of the earth there exists a more ill-used class of men than the London horse-dealers. I am not going to become their champion. I am only desirous of fairly stating their position with regard to many of their customers, on whom their good or bad name mainly depends, leaving my readers, if I have any, to draw their own conclusions therefrom.

A first-rate London dealer buys and sells many hundred horses annually. Nearly all of them he collects at the chief country fairs from their breeders, young, raw, and fleshy, for breeders know better than to knock their young stock about by much riding or exercise. All that is required of a five-year old at a fair, is, that he shall possess freedom of action, be well-shaped, fat, sleek, and unblemished.

After each provincial fair, then, a string of these animals arrives at every London dealer's stable. The dealer can know but little about them individually. Many he has never seen until they reach his premises, they having been purchased by his agents in the country; all he really knows is, that he has spared neither time nor expense in collecting as good a lot as he could, for his own emolument, and his customers' convenience.

If the animals have been judiciously selected, it is probable that, were each horse, when transferred to the stable of a customer, to have fair play, be properly cared for, and not expected to work until his fat had given place to muscle, and until his paces had been confirmed, and his temper corrected by a skilful and patient horseman, the greater number of them would turn out satisfactorily both for buyer and seller. But from the ignorance, meanness, or duplicity both of masters and servants, the reverse too frequently occurs!

I will endeavour to sketch one or two cases which will I think strike every person who has bought and sold horses, as not entirely unfamiliar to him.

Mr. Brown, a gentleman, enters Mr. Snaffle's a dealer's yard. In the first place, Mr. Brown may be an idler, merely desirous of spending an hour amongst horses, and of displaying or improving his equine knowledge at the dealer's expense.

He looks through the stables, causes half a dozen horses to be led out, saddled, mounted, leaped, exerted in every possible manner; and then after finding as many faults as he conveniently can with the animal's paces and shape, he strolls leisurely out of the premises, giving the dealer very fair reason for concluding that he never had the slightest intention of making any purchase at all.

Now, what is ladies' shopping to this? What is the rolling up or refolding a few yards of silk, or calico, compared to drying half-a-dozen inflammatory young horses, excited by the whip and spur almost to madness? Yet if the dealer appears displeased at the gentleman's operations, or unwilling to allow his stables to be turned topsy-turvy for his pastime, Mr. Brown tells all his friends that Snaffle is an insolent rascal, and all Mr. Brown's friends readily believe him, for it is a notorious truism that all horse-dealers are so.

Supposing, however, that Mr. Brown really does want a horse ; if it is to be a hackney, he will probably exact from the dealer a warranty that it can go hunting also ; if he requires a hunter, it must of course be good on the road, and have no striking objections to harness. He will expect him to be as quiet as a sheep, of great courage, beautiful in shape, perfect in action, unblemished, yet experienced in the vicissitudes of the hunting field ; round as a prize pig, yet fit to go to work immediately—and all this at five or six years old.

And if the dealer will warrant his horse to possess, in an eminent degree, all these qualities (and any others which may occur to Mr. Brown on the spur of the moment), Mr. Brown, if he be a liberal fellow, will not object to give a fair market price for the phenomenon, say 105*l*. taking unlimited credit or not, according to his prospects on the Leger.

Having written a cheque for the price agreed upon, and secured such a warranty from the dealer, as he must know, if he be not an idiot, to be an absurdity from beginning to end, Mr. Brown mounts his new purchase and rides it away to test its qualifications.

Now if Mr. Brown be a baddish rider, the first omnibus which occurs settles the question at once; the young horse, although warranted quiet on a half-crown stamp, never having beheld a vehicle of the kind before, is naturally startled at the clatter of the 'infernal machine,' springs across the road, and unships its new owner, who returns on foot to Mr. Snaffle's foaming at the mouth, at what he calls the dealer's rascality in selling him a restive animal.

He does not for a moment consider that it is an utter impossibility for Mr. Snaffle to be thoroughly acquainted with the temper of every horse which passes through his hands; neither does he stop to enquire how far he himself is qualified to conduct a colt through the shows of London. It may here be objected that if a dealer cannot depend on a horse's temper, he ought not to warrant it quiet, but an animal which under one man will be perfectly manageable, is often viewed by another, who does not posess *l'habitude du cheval*, in the light of a wild beast; and anyone in his senses ought to be aware that even a blind jackass might be excused for shying at three omnibuses charging in line, as is 'their custom of an afternoon' in the Edgware Road, or at Punch and Judy, or at one of the advertising locomotives, or at any such like metropolitan peculiarities.

Nevertheless, if Mr. Brown tumbles off and hurts himself, ' the vicious horse which that rascal Snaffle *stuck into him*,'[1] and which would have killed him if he had 'not had the presence of mind to throw himself off,' becomes the hero of his longest after-dinner narrative for life.

Supposing, however, that Mr. Brown does *not* meet an omnibus (a most improbable supposition in these days, I admit) and that he reaches the Park in safety, he first gives his new purchase all manner of walks, trots, and gallops, until the beast is in a lather, 'just to try him;' and finally pulls up at the bleakest corner of Grosvenor Place, to obtain the opinion of two or three of his sporting friends, who opportunely happen to be emerging from Tattersall's at the moment, as to the merits of his new purchase.

[1] N.B.—Mr. Brown chose the horse himself, and he is sure he is a good judge.

Now every sporting man knows, or thinks he knows, a thing or two more than anybody else about horses; at any rate he knows that Mr. Brown does not stop to ask him to point out the *good* qualities of the animal, for if they had not been obvious, of course Mr. Brown would not have been so green as to have purchased it: so the knot of critics set deliberately to work to pick holes in the poor hot, fat, weak thing's coat, whilst the cutting east wind is rapidly cooling it with more expedition than safety.

Though unable to detect any very glaring imperfections in its shape and action, they must be very dull dogs indeed if they cannot succeed in making Mr. Brown uncomfortable by hinting at imperceptible marks on its knees, filmy appearances in its eyes, inequality of action, &c. &c. &c. It is true they do not quite coincide in their criticism; but there is one point on which they are all agreed, viz. 'that Mr. Snaffle is a notorious rascal, that he has taken them all in at various periods of their lives (before they were as clever as they now are), and that they are quite sure that somehow or other he has on the present occasion taken in Mr. Brown also, as Mr. Brown will find very soon to his cost.'

Mr. Brown upon this distrusts his new nag more and more; he begins to look upon it as a locomotive manufactured especially for purposes of deception, by Mr. Snaffle—as a quadruped compounded of spavins, splints, curbs, thrushes, cataracts, navicular diseases, roarings, and all manner of vices and infirmities to which equine nature is heir; he, therefore, returns to the Park, determined to give the brute 'a regular good trial.' He gallops it, trots it, gallops it again. The tired beast begins to stumble, nearly or quite comes down, and disgusts Mr. Brown so much, that by the time he gets it home, he hates the horse for stumbling, himself for buying it, and that villain Snaffle for selling it to him.

Yet the horse may after all be a good horse enough. Though of large frame, and fair shape and action, it is young, weak, and fat; and has never been used to such violent exercise as Mr. Brown's 'trials.'

The next morning Mr. Brown's groom (no friend of Mr. Snaffle's), informs his master that the new horse appears very dull, refuses to feed, and coughs heavily. Mr. Brown forthwith orders him to be saddled once more, and mounts him; but the east wind has done its work; the poor beast is so ill, that it is with difficulty led back to its stable, where it speedily exhibits in perfection all the symptoms of acute inflammation.

Mr. Brown recurs to his warranty, informs Snaffle of the animal's state, and proposes that he shall receive him back into his stable, and return the cheque for 105*l*.

The rascal Snaffle declines to accede to this liberal proposal.

Mr. Brown menaces him with an action.

The villain Snaffle is unmoved by the threat. Meantime the horse dies, and being as fat as a prize pig, fetches a fancy price from the knacker's. Mr. Brown brings his action, and states conscientiously, through his counsel, to an enlightened jury of his countrymen, composed of tailors, shoemakers, seedsmen, and such like estimable nonsporting members of society, what he believes to be the facts of the case.

His groom deposes on oath, that the horse coughed as soon as he entered Mr. Brown's stable, was taken violently ill during the night, and died before the end of the week. For the defence, a few strappers employed in Mr. Snaffle's yard swear stoutly that the horse was perfectly well when he left their stable ; but strappers' oaths being notoriously profane, are not much attended to in courts of law, and Mr. Snaffle is ultimately cast, and has to repay the 105*l.*—*minus* the fancy price which the knackers gave for the dead horse, and *plus* the costs of the action.

All the people who only suspected that Mr. Snaffle was a rascal before the trial, are now quite sure of it ; for he has been pronounced to be one by that impartial tribunal, an intelligent English jury, whose experience of horse-dealing, if they have any, has been acquired at Smithfield, where the prads are more likely to succumb under glanders than inflammation.

The consultation with the sporting gentlemen at the bleak corner of Grosvenor Place, is unknown to Mr. Snaffle, has never been mentioned by Mr. Brown, and would have been scouted by the jury if suggested as the real cause of the horse's death, for *their* horses stand about in their tax-carts in all weathers—and never die of inflammation or fat either.

Such cases as this and worse occur daily to dealers; who, knowing that 'the world is not their friend, nor the world's law,' resign themselves to innumerable losses rather than appear as defendants in a court of justice—I mean in a court of law. Purchasers take themselves in, as Sam Slick says, quite as often as they are taken in by the dealers; and they not unfrequently do so with their eyes open; trusting to the unreasonable warranty which they have wrung from the seller, to furnish them with an excuse for returning the animal they have bought, if they see cause afterwards to repent of their bargain.

Everybody has heard sporting men boast of having sold horses for much larger sums than they originally paid the dealer for them. If a Mr. Brown gives one hundred and five guineas for a hunter, and sells him to Lord Tom Towzel of the Windsor Local Horse for two hundred and fifty, he plumes himself mightily on his sagacity. Yet the dealer who sold him the animal comes in neither for a share of the profit, nor the praise.

But let the same Mr. Brown select a bad horse from the dealer's stud, although he very likely may do so contrary to the man's wishes and advice, and let him afterwards mismanage and maltreat him in his dislike of a beast—whose only fault, perhaps, consists in being of too generous a spirit for its timid owner—no words will then be too strong to express Mr. B.'s spite and indignation, if he loses fifty or sixty pounds by the transaction.

All customers are not like Mr. Brown; but unfortunately a good many are.

Now for a word on veterinary surgeons, the natural enemies of horse-dealers.

A veterinary surgeon, like other tradesmen, must endeavour to give satisfaction to his customers. If Mr. Brown sends a horse to be examined, and the animal be pronounced unsound, he gladly pays Seton, the vet., his half-guinea, and is much obliged to him for having prevented some rascally horse-dealer from cheating him. Mr. Brown forthwith selects another horse (we know that he likes shopping), with which Mr. Seton is equally discontented, Mr. Brown then selects a third, and perhaps Mr. Seton passes that; Mr. Brown is satisfied that the fastidious Mr. Seton is a most careful fellow, and recommends him to all his friends; Mr. Seton is satisfied that he has received a guinea and a half instead of half a guinea; and Mr. Snaffle is satisfied that Mr. Brown has probably picked out the worst horse of the three.

I do not mean to accuse Mr. Seton of wilfully imputing unsoundness to a sound horse—but it is his interest to be *very particular*; and if a vet. chooses to be very particular, he can, conscientiously, pass no horse that ever was foaled. Men are not worked so hard, or so young as horses, yet where is the man who hath not an occasional cough, or corn in his toe, or inequality in his action, or weakness in his eye? which, however, does not prevent his walking like Barclay, riding like Mason, skating like Sheppard, or cricketing like Lillywhite.

No, no, soundness is a very good and desirable thing—but it is not the *only* thing needful in a horse; those who have had much practice in this matter well know. A hack may be a very clever one, yet cough now and then: or he may be perfectly sound, and yet not be worth a shilling for work. A hunter may have thin feet, curbs, splints, and be blemished from head to tail, and yet be sold cheap at three hundred guineas.

I would bet good odds that few of Count D'Orsay's cab-horses, Lord Willoughby D'Eresby's coachers, Lord Anglesey's hacks, or Lord Chesterfield's hunters would pass at any vet.'s in town, without the discovery of some imperfection, which would deter Mr. Brown from buying them of a dealer. Yet, that they are the pick of English horseflesh, nobody will deny.

I will conclude with a few words of advice to the horse-dealing public; which some of them may be more likely to follow, from my assuring them in the first place that I don't care twopence whether they do or not.

To a purchaser I would suggest, that he should study attentively Sam Slick's chapter on horse-dealing. Caveat Emptor's work is witty—but it is like Accum's 'Analysis of Wines,' such an exaggeration, that if either were closely attended to, men would nowhere find horses sound enough to ride, or wine pure enough to drink. In the next place, let him not expect to get a horse worth 200*l.* for half the money. If he does attempt any such 'artful dodge,' surely the dealer in self-defence is justified in charging him 100*l.* for one only worth 50*l.*

Let him recollect that no man ever had good horses unless he had a good groom, a good stable, good provender, and a good supply of it. Let him not set himself down as a dupe on discovering faults in a new purchase, which he did not observe in the dealer's yard. The horse may have a dozen faults undiscovered by both buyer and seller at the time of sale, and yet be worth double the money paid for it; or it may have none at all—apparent ones, I mean—and yet be of a weakly constitution, or a faint spirit. Finally, let him bear in mind, that

> 'Every species of ground every horse does not suit :
> What at Quorn's a good hunter, may here prove a brute :'

which means, in prosaic language, that a good horse *out of his place*, will not prove so satisfactory a purchase as a very moderate one which *is in his place*; that the best hack in England would cut a poor figure in a quick fifty minutes over deep grass, whilst the famous Lottery might probably be considered dear at 50*l.* by a man who wished merely for a showy nag on which to do dandy in Rotten Row.

CORNET RAG AND CAPTAIN FAMISH.

CORNET RAG and Captain Famish are average specimens of two sorts of Military tigers who may be seen any Monday at Tattersall's, or at any steeple-chase, or congregated in groups on horseback about five o'clock during the London season under the trees by the side of the Serpentine, examining with much interest the suspicious-looking inmates of the flashy broughams which parade up and down 'the Light Ladye's mile.'

Cornet Rag is a small dapper Yorkshire man. He went when very young into a crack light cavalry regiment, and before he was twenty, had cheated all his brother officers so infernally, selling them lame horses for sound ones, and winning their money by all manner of quaint and ingenious contrivances, that his Colonel advised him to retire, which he very speedily did, getting an unusually high price for his commission, and accommodating the youngster who succeeded him, with a glandered charger at an uncommonly stiff figure.

He has since devoted his time to billiards, steeple-chasing, and the turf. His head-quarters are Rummer's in Conduit Street, where he keeps his kit, but he is ever on the move, travelling about the country in the exercise of his vocation, as a gentleman jockey and gentleman leg.

According to Bell's Life he is a regular attendant at every race, and an actor in most of them. He rode the winner at Northampton, he was left for dead a fortnight ago in a ditch at Harrow, and yet there he was last week at the Bois de Berny, pale and determined as ever, astonishing the badauds of Paris by the neatness of his rig, and the elegance of his seat as he took a preliminary gallop on that vicious brute 'Scroggins' before starting for 'the French Grand National.'

He did not win the race. Everybody knew that, but he won 1800*l*. by losing it, which suited him much better. Everbody does not know that, luckily for Cornet Rag.

He does not play billiards often, and never in

public; but when he does play, he always gets hold of a good flat, and never leaves him till he has done him uncommonly brown.

He is a constant attendant at 'the corner,' where he compiles a limited but comfortable libretto. During the season he rides often in the Park, mounted on a clever lean hack; he is generally to be seen escorting that celebrated horsewoman, Fanny Highflier, or in confidential converse with that eminent handicapper and statesman, Lord Thimblerig.

Though tolerably well connected, he eschews civilised society, and would rather dine off a steak at the One Tun, with Sam Snaffle, Captain O'Rourke, and two or three other notorious turf robbers, than with the choicest company in London.

He likes to boast at Rummer's that he is going to run down and spend his Saturday and Sunday with his friend Hocus, the leg, at his little box near Epsom, where, if report speaks true, many rummish plants are concocted.

When he does make his appearance in ladies' society, which occasionally occurs at a hunt meeting or a race ball, he talks to them briskly about the proper pace at which to ride a refuser at timber, or instructs them as to the most judicious mode of putting a kicker in harness. He is rather popular amongst women of a lower grade, he is so confident and smart, and looks so well in his scarlet satin jacket and doe skins, and rides so gallantly.

His friend, Captain Famish, is a tiger of a very different kidney. He is a tall, gaunt, pale cockney, who has perhaps served for a couple of years in some regiment of Heavy Dragoons.

He now, however, has retired, and devotes himself entirely, after his fashion, to dress and the ladies. He does not know many of the latter, and would have little to say to them if he did, for he is a dull dog; but he follows them about at public places, and ogles them lugubriously, trusting much to the fascination of his glance, and to his greasy hair and dyed moustaches, and above all to the general emaciation of his appearance.

He either drives about a badly hung, showy cab, drawn by a great, staring, grey horse with grand action before and none behind, or else prances along on a leggy, fat beast with a small head and a big tail, and no action at all either before or behind, which the dealer who sold it called 'a werry charger-like looking os.' He dines often at the Wyndham or in Baker Street, where his title of Captain gives him a sort of importance. The young ladies of that region consider his debauched, unwholesome look interesting.

He is to be often seen in private boxes at theatres, accompanied by mysterious females crouching back behind the silk curtains. He takes intense and obtrusive interest in the '*succés*' of the columbine at Drury Lane.

He is a serious nuisance to such of his neighbours as chance to have pretty nursery maids.

His dress is peculiar. His trousers are extraordinarily capacious, covering his whole foot save his big toe nail, which is resplendent with French polish. They are composed of a sort of Tartan-monstre of most exaggerated pattern and hues, his coat is low-collared, loose and devoid of padding, his throat open, he wears a narrow riband in lieu of a cravat.

He frequents Rummer's, too, but does not take such an active part in sporting events as his friend and companion Cornet Rag. I am not sorry to say that he got horribly thrashed the other day by an uxorious baker whose domestic felicity he was endeavouring to disturb.[1]

When he has recovered from his black eyes and swollen nose, and when Cornet Rag has returned from Paris, where he is now swaggering about the Boulevards, you may see this precious pair of tigers, or two others exactly like them, any day you chance to look out in the Park for their great ill-appointed flashy cab.

The wretched child behind it does not appear to have been weaned many months, and would be much more in his place at an infant school, than in those shamefully tight leather breeches.

---

[1] To do Famish justice, he behaved quite like a *gentleman* on the occasion. He sent a *friend* to the baker, who in the most ruffianly manner would have thrashed him too, had he not rapidly placed himself under the protection of B 27.

CAPTAIN JACK.

IN the year 1823 I was employed as overseer on the east coast of the river Demerary in South America. Early in that year an insurrection broke out amongst the negroes, and the white servants on the estates were assembled at Stabrock, the capital of the colony, embodied into a corps of riflemen, and brigaded in different parts of the country with the regular troops.

It so happened that I was stationed with several companies of the ——th regiment, commanded by Colonel ——, close to the property on which I had for several years resided. I was thereby enabled to be of considerable use to the military authorities on several occasions, from my intimate knowledge of the localities of the neighbourhood, and of the character of the people by whom we were surrounded.

The communications between the plantations on the coast and the town of Stabroek, is kept up by small schooners, which carry thither weekly the produce ready for shipping on board the merchantmen in the river, and return laden with coals, provisions, and other necessary supplies.

These droghers, as they are called, are manned and commanded by negroes; to be a boat captain is a situation of great trust and emolument, which is always filled by the best man on each estate. These boat captains contrive to pick up a good deal of money by carrying letters and passengers, the profit arising from which is their perquisite.

Whenever I had occasion to go to town, I generally gave the preference to a schooner belonging to Plantation Eugenia; she was the fastest boat on the coast, and her commander, Captain Jack, was a smart, active, well-behaved fellow, whose popularity with white and black stood him in good stead; for whenever it was known that the Eugenia's schooner was to sail, the other droghers had but small chance of passengers.

On one unlucky evening, soon after the insurrection broke out, Captain Jack returned from Stabroek, with his boat full of strange negroes who were cordially welcomed in the negro yard of the Eugenia.

That very night, the dwelling house of Mr. Forester, the proprietor of the estate, was attacked and burnt to the ground, and he himself only escaped at the time, to die shortly afterwards of a fever brought on by the hardships he had been forced to undergo in concealing himself from his quick-sighted enemies. For two days he lay without food or shelter in the cotton pieces, exposed to the scorching sun and heavy dews of a tropical climate, and at night he waded along the sea-shore, up to his neck in mud and water, until he reached the house of a friend near town, where he expired in a few days.

Colonel —— wished to send notice of this outrage to the officer commanding at Stabroek, and as Captain Jack's character was above suspicion, he selected him to convey the express to town, and sent a sergeant on horseback to direct him to prepare to weigh immediately.

The man rode to the Eugenia, and went on

board the schooner, which was lying high and dry on the sand. There was nobody in charge of her, her sails and rigging were cut to pieces, her rudder burnt, her anchor and chain gone. Captain Jack was nowhere to be found. The soldier returned to Mahaica port, and made his report. Colonel —— sent for me. He told me that he was aware I was well acquainted with Jack; and that he was informed a sort of friendship existed between us, if, indeed, in those days, a friendship could be said to exist between a negro and a white man, that I knew his haunts and connections, and that if anybody could find him I could. He said he was now convinced that Jack was implicated in the crime committed on Plantation Eugenia, and that he would give me fifty dollars to produce him, dead or alive, before night.

At this period the very existence of the colony was in a most critical position, the numerical odds against the whites were as fifty to one; the negroes equalled us in courage and surpassed us in animal strength and endurance; on the other hand, we were better armed, and possessed that confidence in each other, so essential in the hour of danger.

We had also in the colony the regiment which Colonel —— commanded and a small detachment of artillery.

From circumstances which had occurred during my residence on the east coast, I had acquired such a regard for poor Jack, that I declare I would sooner have been instrumental in arresting any white man in the colony: with the conviction, which I had in this case, that his death would be the inevitable consequence of his apprehension. Still, this was no time for a man to swerve from his duty, however painful it might be: horrible atrocities had been committed by the insurgent negroes, and signal must be the punishment inflicted on the perpetrators, whenever they could be discovered.

I therefore shouldered my rifle, and sallied forth, determined to do my best to apprehend Jack, not without a hope, I confess, that his well-known activity and sagacity might render my exertions fruitless.

I had scarcely walked half a mile, when at an angle of the road I came full on the very man of whom I had been sent in quest. I at once sprang forward and seized him by the throat. His astonishment at this unfriendly greeting from me, was so great that he made no resistance whatever. My uniform showed him that I was on duty, and his conscience probably apprised him of the cause of this hostile proceeding on my part.

'Colonel —— has sent for you, Jack,' said I; 'I trust you will be able to account for the state in which your boat was found, when he wished you to take his despatches to town.'

Jack made no reply, but shook his head mournfully. I motioned to him to walk on before me towards the military post. He did so. Presently, he stopped, and turned round. Seeing that I unslung and cocked my rifle, he said :—

'Massa Edward, s'pose Jack run away, you no shoot him?'

'That I most certainly will, Jack. I have been ordered to convey you dead or alive to Mahaica, and dead or alive you shall go thither. I am sorry for you from the bottom of my heart, for I am sure you have been unwillingly compelled to join in the destruction of Mr. Forester's property.'

We soon reached the post, where I delivered over my prisoner to the guard. He was instantly taken before Colonel —— and several other officers, and I lingered in the guard-room, ostensibly for the purpose of reposing myself, but really to see how my poor friend Jack would fare. After some time had elapsed, I grew tired of waiting, and was walking out of the gate, when Colonel —— advanced to the front of the gallery before the officers' apartments, and exclaimed in an angry tone,

'Where the devil are you going to, sir? How dare you leave your prisoner without orders?'

'I thought, Colonel, that my duty had been ended when I delivered my prisoner to the guard.'

'Did you, by G—, sir? Remain where you are, and I'll soon convince you of the contrary.'

He then returned into the house for a short time, and reappeared followed by the other officers, and by Jack, who walked slowly down the steps towards me. The colonel and his friends remained above, leaning over the front of the gallery.

'Now, Sergeant Willes,' continued Colonel ——, 'place your prisoner on his knees, with his face towards you.'

Jack knelt down, not a muscle of his countenance quivered, he was entirely naked, and was a remarkably muscular and finely made man. He looked like a beautiful bronze statue. Both he and I knew perfectly well that his life was forfeited and that he was about to die, but we were neither of us prepared for what followed.

'Fall back six paces!' roared Colonel ——. I obeyed.

'*Now, shoot your prisoner through the heart.*'

I was horror-stricken. Well aware that poor Jack's hours were numbered, I had never contemplated the possibility of being compelled, myself, thus to become his executioner in cold blood. I knew, moreover, that Colonel —— had no right to make me carry the sentence of the drum-head court-martial into effect. I was a civilian, a volunteer, and a non-commissioned officer, and from the various services which my local knowledge had enabled me to render him, I had no reason to expect such brutal treatment at his hands. As soon as I had sufficiently recovered from my astonishment and horror, I advanced towards the gallery in order to remonstrate. He turned away from me, and called to the officer of the guard to send two men with loaded muskets forward.

The men stepped out, and, at his command, cocked their pieces and levelled them at me.

Colonel —— then said to them, 'I am going to give my orders to that damned mutineer. If he does not obey them instantly, shoot him. *Now*, Sergeant Willes, make ready, present, fire.'

Jack sprang to his feet, and fell stone dead. My bullet had pierced his brain.

Colonel —— tossed the purse containing the reward offered for Jack's apprehension on the ground, close by his dead body, and sauntered coolly into the house, observing, that until the Volunteers and Indians formed some idea of military discipline from experience, they would give more trouble than assistance to the Regulars.

He lived to see the day when he gladly would have exchanged his whole regiment for a score of our good rifles; yet he lived not long. Three days after the tragedy which I have here related, he attempted, against the advice of the colonists, to pursue a body of negroes into the bush, with the whole force at Mahaica, unaccompanied either by Volunteers or Indians. His men, encumbered by their heavy clothing and accoutrements, exhausted by the heat, and bewildered by the heavy torrents of rain which flooded the savannahs and rendered the creeks impassable, fell an easy prey to their naked and agile enemies. Not more than a dozen escaped to tell the tale of their defeat. Colonel —— received a musket-shot which broke both his thighs. He fell alive into the hands of his enemies.

They had been Captain Jack's comrades and friends, and horribly they avenged his death.

SPORTING TIGERS.

THE term 'sporting man' is a wide one. It may mean either Lord George Bentinck owner of a string of a hundred race horses, and standing to win or lose 50,000*l.* on the event of a race, or it may be applied with equal aptness to the spirited proprietor of the Staffordshire Dentist, who is open to match his dog against anything alive under forty pounds in weight, for a fair scratch fight, and whose money is to be heard of at the Dog and Duck, Leek, Potteries.

It may be predicated of Thomas Spring, champion of England, or of an octogenarian cripple desirous of showing a black-and-tan spaniel under five pounds, for three qualities, against any other black-and-tan existing. It may be affirmed of an expert cudgel-player, or of an astute thimble-rigger; it may be used offensively or in admiration. I really find myself unable to define in the abstract, what 'a sporting man' is. Pickpockets are sporting men, dog fighters and fanciers, dove butchers, tato-all-hot men who dispose of their viands by means of round-abouts, legs of every grade, hell-keepers, and gents on the turf are all 'sporting men.' Very few real sportsmen are 'sporting men.'

The peculiar class of which I mean to treat in the present paper, forms, perhaps, the most amusing and least offensive species of the whole genus.

They have been considerably diminished in number by the introduction of steam, and in order to do them justice I must entreat my readers to allow me to carry their imaginations back a few years to the period when coaching was in its zenith. I will call them, for distinction's sake, 'the London Sporting Tigers.'

An individual of this species may be known at once by his dress; the only possible mistake that can be made in judging of him in this way, may be in taking him for an opulent book-keeper at a coach office, or for an omnibus cad who has inherited a fortune.

He usually wears a broadish-brimmed hat,

furnished with a loop and string to secure it to his head in tempestuous weather, and a long-waisted dark coat, with a widish hem in lieu of a collar, and with astoundingly wide-apart hind buttons, very loose and ample in the skirts; his neck-cloth is generally white, and tied so as to display as much of his poll as possible; his waistcoat is easy, long, and groomish in cut, whilst his trousers are close-fitting, short, and secured under a thick round-toed well-cleaned boot by a long narrow strap. His great coat, wrapper, coatoon, pea jacket, or whatever he may please to call it, is indescribable, bepatched bestitched and bepocketed most unaccountably, and constructed on the plan best calculated to afford extraordinary facilities for getting at half-pence to pay turnpikes with rapidity, and for withstanding unusual inclemency of weather in an exposed situation. There is an affectation of premature senility in his dress and demeanour, an ostentatious disregard of popular prejudice and established custom; the useful evidently predominating therein over the usual.

The Sporting Tiger saunters along with a sort of jaunty swagger, twitching his head on one side about thrice every minute; he carries a slight switch in his hand, with which he deliberately rehearses, as he strolls along, the outline of a severe double thonging with which he means to surprise his team when he sets one up. The best specimens of this interesting animal are to be met with loitering between Bond street and Conduit street after three o'clock. Earlier than that they congregate in the Regent Circus to see the Brighton coaches start, or at least they did so before the Brighton Railway opened.

What on earth the destitute creatures will do now of a morning I cannot imagine, unless, like the Naval captain, they betake themselves to the study of Steam.

The Sporting Tiger converses most willingly of prize-fights, steeple-chases, hounds and racing, not as a principal in those exciting recreations, but as a man who has had his day, and can now, with experienced eye and chastened passions, look philosophically on, and smile indulgently at the errors committed by less wide awake young 'uns.

But what appears to interest him above all things in this sublunary scene are the family affairs of stage-coachmen, and the success or failure of the coaches committed to their charge.

He would rather be accosted familiarly before witnesses by Brighton Bill than by the Duke of Wellington; he knows to a sixpence how much per mile the proprietors of the 'Age' divided last month, and how many horses they lost in the great snow; he presents whips as pledges of friendship to his coaching pals, inscribed with Spartan brevity on a silver band around the handle: 'James Green to Roger Slugpunisher' or perhaps more mysteriously, thus :—' A real Brick to a real Brick.'

He knows accurately the terms these men are on with their employers, and talks of Messrs. Chaplin and Horne, the great coach proprietors, as of respectable and wealthy, but capricious and severe individuals. Railroads he considers as devilish innovations, and prophesies obscurely the advent of a sort of coaching millennium, when boilers shall burst, and trains run off the rail spontaneously by Divine interposition in favour of Mr. Roger Slugpunisher and his fellow 'bricks.'

If a Sporting Tiger owns a horse he generally drives it. He rarely buys it of a dealer, but rather 'out of a coach.' He willingly details to you how his skewbald mare kicked so infernally that Tom Crop threatened to resign his seat on the 'Magnet,' if he was expected to sit behind her; how he (the Sporting Tiger) purchased her for twenty-one pounds five shillings (she looks worth ten) and took and put her into a gig and drove her slap down to Richmond, and how the discerning mare eschewed kicking when she found she had a chap behind her that would stand no nonsense.

At other times he discourses of a cropped horse which Jack Territ vowed was 'wored out,' and which he, therefore, contrived to pick up for 'a song,' after which the cropped horse picked up also, turned out to be only just 'six off;' and for which the Sporting Tiger would not take ninety guineas if they were laid down on the table before him, a temptation to which he is not likely to be exposed, if the cropped horse's appearance be any criterion of its value.

He is proud of the style of his driving, considers his seat on a coach-box as unexceptionable, and his manner of wielding the whip inimitable both for grace and severity. He flatters himself that his whistle is an unfailing diuretic, and he is an undoubted proficient in those indescribable, guttural grunts, smacks, and clicks, which appear from their results to be so stimulating to the paces and grating to the feelings of the genus Equus.

Behind one of his animals in a buggy, or, perhaps, both in a phaeton, without bearing reins, and with chain trace ends and pole pieces, the Sporting Tiger rattles down to the circus to see the 'Age' start. He details to the first stray porter or book-keeper who has leisure to listen to him the birth, parentage, education and future prospects of his prads; he comments upon any perceptible change in the team of the coach with as much interest as if it were a change in the Cabinet; he enquires anxiously concerning the state of the roads, and learns with concern that they are woolly below Crawley, although he has no intention of going thither.

If the 'Age' be 'light out' he sends home his vehicle in charge of his scrubby groom—whom he has selected, as well as his horses, out of some coaching stable—and accompanies the coach as far as 'the Elephant' or 'the Bricklayers' in order to pick up an idea or two, and cultivate the driver's intimacy.

In his hotel he is confidential with the head waiter—with whom he bets occasionally on races—and familiar with the subordinates. He seeks to nourish himself on the food which would be most likely to suit the manly palate of a jockey or a boxer, breaking his fast with a red herring and a pint of purl, or with porter and an underdone beefsteak. He sneers at bread and butter as effeminate, and sets down an individual who drinks tea as a spoon. He would rather pass his evening with a 'tramp' who would floor his liquors like a man and say nothing, than with the most agreeable teetotaller that ever quenched his thirst with toast and water.

Nevertheless I cannot say that I have observed that this studiously masculine diet causes him to ride harder, drive with more nerve, or excel more obviously in exercises of skill or strength than his more graminivorous and water-drinking contemporaries. He smokes too, like a steamer, and announces daily to the public in his coffee-room, that one havannah after breakfast is to him a necessary of life.

He never goes into ladies' society, if he can avoid so doing, agreeing with Roger Slugpunisher in the apophthegm, that ' women is rum stock.' He therefore is only acquainted with the females of his own family—whom he fights shy of as much as possible—and with such as he falls in with at the theatres and the oyster saloon. From a close and careful investigation of the characteristics of the latter, he has, as he conceives, acquired a thorough insight into the female disposition in general, to all the dodges of which he avers that he is fully up.

He enjoys a dog-fight, and delights in a set-to, provided he be not a principal in the business, unless, indeed, great superiority in strength or skill be on his side. If he has a preference for any particular pastime, it may be said to be for twisting off a knocker in peace and quiet, or for mobbing a policeman. The latter relaxation, however, he only allows himself under very favourable circumstances, when the patient appears to be a weakly individual, and when he himself is supported by a strong body of muscular friends.

His evenings are mostly passed at the cider cellar, or in brandy-and-watering at the bar of his own hotel.

His only literary employment consists in regulating a small oval betting book. If he speaks the truth, the whole truth and nothing but the truth, he is deeply concerned in every important event which comes off either on the turf or in the ring; and twice in each year he enacts for a few days the character of a ruined man or a millionaire according to the result of the weighty bets which he gives out that he has depending on the Derby or the Leger.

He prides himself on possessing the friendship and support of the most distinguished jockeys and trainers of the day, whom he occasionally entertains with much magnificence at the 'One Tun' in Jermyn Street.

A race course is his elysium, the Epsom week, the bright spot in his annual existence. The Moulsey course is, however, perhaps, better adapted to the calibre of the Sporting Tiger. He is there a triton amongst minnows. He has, possibly, a rip of his own to start for the hack stakes, or, at least, has a friend who has one. He walks up the course in mysterious conference with some well-known raffish steeple-chase rider, leaning on the neck of his pony.

For his own riding, he prefers a tight cob to a horse, the shorter its tail the better. In opposition to most mortals, he takes off his straps before mounting, and exhibits a lounging seat with very short stirrups. He usually carries a natty zephyr waterproof strapped in front of his saddle, not to be taken alive in case of rain.

Although convinced himself, and flattering himself that he has convinced others, that he can at will distinguish himself in whatever line he may undertake, he unfortunately persists in undertaking nothing at all; and as tailors', tobacconists' and livery stable and inn-keepers' bills, *vires acquirunt cundo*, the Sporting Tiger is removed, after a season, from the purlieux of Bond Street to the Rules of the Bench, where he speedily adapts himself to circumstances, plays at racquets and drinks beer incessantly, wears out his old clothes, and cultivates chin wigs, charlies and mustachios to such a luxuriant extent that his heaviest creditors can scarcely recognise him, when they look in upon him of a morning to see that he is safe.

The Elephant and Castle being nearly within the Rules, he is thereby enabled to see something of the coaching world without breaking bounds, and he occasionally meets an old sporting friend or two at the cheapest and best whip maker's in England, who also resides hard by.

The Sporting Tiger eventually takes the benefit of the Act, an operation which rather elevates him in the estimation of all such of his associates as do not lose money by him. He generally gets remanded for the full term that the law permits, notwithstanding the consummate dexterity with which his schedule is manufactured, it being a matter of notoriety in the sporting circles that Messrs. Commissioners Fane and Fonblanque are sadly prejudiced men, inimical to the race of tigers in general.

A Sporting Tiger seldom marries; when he does so commit himself, he leads to the altar either a barmaid, a cigariste, or a grisette. I have not yet been able to trace his habits in married life.

Those that do not marry, eventually go abroad. Brussels, Baden Baden, Calais and Boulogne are full of them. I am not quite certain what becomes of such as remain in England, but I rather think that those corpulent elderly gentlemen who infest billiard tables, shooting galleries and hells, apparently more for the sake of society than business, but who don't entirely object to a small bet with a greenhorn or to a little mild, impromptu chicken-hazard when there is nothing else doing on the board of green cloth, must have been in their younger days members of the confraternity of Sporting Tigers.

THE BREAKDOWN.

A Scene under my Windows in Whitehall, 1836.

RAIN, rain, rain—settled, unceasing rain, varying only from the insinuating drizzle to the drenching shower.

In the midst of a most tremendous downpour which for the last half-hour had completely cleared the streets, a crowd is gradually congregating to witness the resurrection of a jaded skeleton of a hackney-coach horse which, hardly able to totter along when on its legs, now that it has fallen, evinces no signs of ever rising again.

There the wretched brute lies, stretched at length in the mud, with glassy upturned eye and clenched teeth, apparently at its last gasp.

A moist and motley assemblage—jarvies, cads, soldiers, pickpockets, and respectables of both sexes, not forgetting a fair proportion of women with babies, who, to do them justice, are ever to be seen foremost in danger in a London crowd, press in upon the prostrate animal, disregarding rain, mud, omnibuses, and their own business if they have any, to gratify themselves with a peep at the poor devil who, certainly, never before, even in his best days, elicited so much attention.

The oil-skin hats and capes of a couple of policemen bob about in the thickest of the crowd. They are evidently very active officers. By their praiseworthy exertions a ring is formed; the horse is denuded of his harness, a ponderous lifeguardsman sitting very unnecessarily on his head during the operation; and a muscular cabman, selected from the adjoining rank for the vigour of his arm, and the peculiarly effective condition of his pigwhip, 'having kindly volunteered his services,' as the playbills have it, steps forward and lashes the fallen horse over the belly and quarters, determined, as he energetically avers, 'to flog the beggar up.'

The spectators encourage him with cheers and laughter, till, perceiving that the poor creature takes no heed of the blows, and apparently does not feel them, they become suddenly touched with pity, cry shame on the operator, and commence a lecture on humanity.

As yet no progress has been made towards setting the languid patient on his legs. The pelting shower precludes the possibility of testing an experiment suggested by a philosophical butcher's boy as very efficacious in similar cases—the application of a wisp of ignited straw to some part of the sufferer's body undefended by hair. Humanity and the rain forbid the trial of such a restorative. All the straw at hand is too wet to burn.

By this time the crowd has increased threefold, so has the rain. The windows in the vicinity are thronged with spectators.

The hackney coach has been shoved out of the way, close to the kerbstone, and the fallen horse's companion in drudgery, cast loose from the pole, is most unfeelingly tugging away at some musty hay tied under the dicky, utterly unmoved by his fellow-labourer's mishap.

Two or three omnibus drivers have pulled up to gratify themselves and their passengers with a sight of what is going on. They are very sarcastic in their remarks on the condition and quality of Jarvy's cattle, and unaffectedly delighted at seeing that there are worse brutes in the world than those whom it is their own lot to torment.

A good many Members on their way to the House have mingled with the throng, and Mr. B. B. Cabbell has alighted from his brougham, and is endeavouring to swarm up a lamp post, in order to direct from that elevated station in society the exertions of Jarvy and his friends. There is nothing like having an experienced commander. This well-known philanthropist, ever alive to the calls of humanity, has already this morning assisted at the extinction of two fires at Pentonville, and was now on his way to preside at the digging out of a Swiss governess and twenty-seven young ladies who had been buried alive by the fall of a stack of chimneys at Balham Hill, when it occurred to him that his presence might be useful here. Prompt as lightning, he has seated himself on the lamp post.

Jarvy, animated by the good M. P.'s patronage, strips off his upper benjamin, determined to do or die. He clearly sees that it will never do to stand inactive under such a shower of rain and jokes as is now pelting him.

His manly form, when divested of his cumbrous upper garment, is set off to advantage by a close-fitting jersey frock, and a pair of black kersey shorts, his legs and ancles are swathed in neatly wrought haybands; his head is defended by a spicy wide-awake, singularly becoming to his open Saxon countenance.

He seizes his unconscious horse by what little tail he has, and tugs with desperate vigour. The aged and experienced waterman pertaining to the stand hard by, cursing awfully, places the animal's legs in what he considers to be the most advantageous position for active exertion.

Policeman B27 jerks the bridle and raps the poor brute over the skull with his staff, in a manner which proves that he is more accustomed to deal with inebriated Irishmen than with half-starved horses.

The commiserating bystanders kick him in the ribs and swear at him.

All this produces no effect. He is, just for a moment, half raised by main strength without any corresponding effort of his own ; but he falls back again heavily on his side, apparently dead.

He *must* be dead. He *is* dead. No. Suddenly he arouses himself, gives a desperate plunge, rises, falls on his knees again, rises once more with a wonderful effort, staggers forward a few paces, knocking B27 head over heels into the mud, and then with reeking hide and drooping head and ears, stands stock-still as if nothing unusual had befallen him.

The crowd, after a roar of laughter at B27's mishap, disperses. A humane bystander absconds with the cruel cabman's pig whip ; the cruel cabman avenges himself by casting a handful of mud at Mr. B. B. C. ; and that philanthropic individual slipping nimbly from his perch, jumps into his brougham and hurries off to the assistance of the sufferers at Balham Hill, carrying with him the approval of his own conscience, and several hearty curses from the bereaved cab driver.

The omnibuses, which, by way of being sociable had drawn up three abreast, so as effectually to impede the thoroughfare—and why, we pause to enquire, should they not do so in a land of liberty?

—gallop off best pace, knocking down, providentially, only one old woman apiece.

In less than a minute the only person to be seen in the street is the Jarvy, who, having resumed his box coat, is proceeding with Britannic calmness to repair his harness.

His *sang froid* is equal to that of his horse. He looks as if what I have attempted to describe were an every-day occurrence to both of them.

Reader, I fear it is so.

THE COURIER.

WE fondly imagine that our tight little island produces everything which it does produce in the very highest perfection. There lives not the lukewarm Briton who can quench his thirst in the 'bière de Mars,' dine on 'bifstcks au beurre d'anchois' at a Parisian café, or gallop a nag, sprung from the 'Razza del Re' up the Strada Nova at Naples without a sigh, expressed or understood, for the very superior articles of the same species which he could enjoy were he in England, through the intervention of Messrs. Barclay and Perkins, Giblett, or Tilbury. The sight of a German postilion conducting six stallions down hill at a banging trot, and at the same time executing a villanously complicated solo on his unwieldy horn, fails to convince an Englishman, as he ought to be convinced, that any continental coachmanship can compare with that of Jack Peer or the Brighton Baronet, although even those Homers do occasionally nod, and deteriorate their passengers' precious limbs occasionally; and the finest bunch of grapes ever grown at Fontainebleau is surpassed in his mind's eye by the costly efforts of his own Scotch forcing gardener. He cannot bring himself to believe that any foreigner breathing the breath of life can back a horse as skilfully as his own diminutive groom; or that a butler is to be found without the white cliffs of Albion capable of decanting port wine as steadily, or burnishing plate as brightly, as his own apoplectic but trustworthy factotum.

As to the relative merits of insular and continental cooks, if our patriot enjoy a good digestion, and be free from gout, he will perhaps liberally allow that it is an open question; that though turtle soup, haunches of venison, and plum pudding are unquestionably edibles of the first class, still much may be adduced in favour of potages à la bisque, turbôt à la crème, and orange flower soufflets.

Much of this sturdy patriotism is reasonable enough. We are unquestionably very lucky fellows, and enjoy at least our due proportion of the good things of this life.

I am fully alive to the potency of our ale, the succulency of our beef and mutton, and the surpassing qualities of our horses, neither would I willingly be supposed to detract in any way from the well-merited reputations of Jack Peer and Sir Vinny. I believe firmly that the only objection to be raised against our hot-house grapes is, that they now and then cost us a guinea a pound. Neither do I deny that our grooms do stick to their saddles like wax, and that, as a nation, our spoons are cleaned better and brighter than those of any other civilised country under the sun. Our domestics are in many points super-excellent, but still, in my humble opinion, they lack the one thing needful for the establishment of a poor man; they want that versatility of talent which distinguishes their continental brethren, and more especially the Swiss and Italians, which two nations chiefly supply that class of travelling servants called couriers.

A courier, to attain eminence in his profession,

must combine in his own person innumerable qualifications. He must be strong, inured to fatigue, a light weight and a good rider; he must possess a smattering of coach-making and cookery, be a thorough valet, understand waiting at table, be expert at accounts, and speak fluently, at least, four or five languages.

We will suppose you, gentle reader, to have landed safely at Calais, and taken up your quarters at the Hôtel du Bourbon Condé. M. Rignolle, the worthy proprietor, in answer to your enquiries about a courier who has been recommended to you, responds, 'he ver nice leetle man, I send for him.' The 'ver nice leetle man' who resembles one of the bettermost kind of Italian princes by whom the Travellers' is infested, arrives, and engages to serve you in every possible sort of way for the sum of eight guineas a month.

He produces a pile of certificates from his former employers, which at once attest the excellence of his character and the richness of the English language; inasmuch as the authors of them appear to have vied with one another in expressing the same feelings in different words.

Lord Warington declares himself highly gratified with the attentive services of Gioacchino Bruschetti, and confirms the document with his aristocratic coat of arms, which the warmth of Gioacchino's breeches' pocket has converted into a daub of red wax.

Messrs. Hobbs and Dobbs assure future travellers that Bruschetti is a capital fellow, and a real treasure to any person wishing to travel speedily through France and Italy. They also confirm their autographs with their seals, which, having been fellow-passengers with Lord Warington's, for once, look equally imposing.

On the morning of your departure from Calais you observe a man arrayed in a gorgeously braided military jacket, yellow leather tights and slippers, busying himself in the superintendence of the loading of your carriage. In him you recognise the real treasure to persons wishing to travel speedily. He forthwith assumes the command, hands you into your britschka, bundles the lady's maid into the rumble, starts the whole equipage, pays the bills, shakes hands with the waiters, kisses M. Rignolle on both whiskers, and jingles by you on his *bidet*, merrily smacking his whip, in order to get the horses ready for you at the next relay, where he is well known to and cordially greeted by the post boys, who feel assured that they have in him, if they drive their best, and half murder their master's horses, a steady advocate for '*trois francs par poste, et la goutte*,' equivalent to about sixpence a mile with us.

At some *postes*, however, where he has met with vexatious delay on former journeys, or been furnished with a foundered *bidet*, he is not quite so popular. The postilions recollect his having rigidly adhered to the tariff in remunerating their tardy services; or perhaps the *maître de poste* may call to mind stern battles on the subject of the '*troisième cheval*' or the age of some miraculously fine child alleged to be under the age of six years, in which our sharp friend Gioacchino proved the better man.

In the same breath he will generally reassure the ladies, who may possibly feel alarmed at the steepness of the road or the absence of '*gardefous*,' and then fulminate a torrent of incoherent blasphemy against the dilatory post boys, which you could not help smiling at, if you understood it, on account of its absurdity.

In countries where avant-couriers are obsolete, he will lay aside his military costume, strap his saddle and jack boots on the imperial, and accompany the lady's maid in the rumble. Here he endeavours to make up for the time lost in relaying by what he calls '*pousser les postillons*,' an operation evidently based on the principle of whipping the willing horse. The faster they drive the more vociferously he urges them on. No matter whether you are pressed for time or not, his credit requires that you should be driven best pace. A slow sulky conductor he silently endures, and tariffs him accurately on reaching the end of the stage, observing laconically '*come si va così si paga.*'

Few people can conscientiously assert that they have known their courier to eat, drink, or sleep whilst on the road. He has no time for so doing, if he should be so irregular as to so wish it.

On reaching your destination for the night, he has to select the most eligible rooms, jockey the other travellers if he can, get fires lit, unload the carriage, air the beds, superintend the supper, and not unfrequently cook it. When you retire to rest he must attend you as a valet, see your clothes and boots cleaned, examine the state of the carriage and have any necessary repairs executed, procure fresh milk and butter for your early breakfast, order the horses, call you in the morning—generally two or three times,—repack the luggage, fight with the innkeeper on the subject of overcharges, satisfy the servants, look after the lady's maid, and be ready to start as soon as you are ; and all this he must repeat daily whilst you are on your journey, besides galloping some seventy or eighty miles on such hacks as it may please Providence and the post-masters to provide him with.

We once, and only once, detected our courier partaking of a slight picnic in the dicky with the maid, and that was probably more from a desire to ingratiate himself with her (for she was very pretty, and, alas ! a pretty Abigail is a rock on which many of the most eminent of couriers have split,) than from any unprofessional habit of eating and drinking, on his part.

If, however, he is overworked whilst travelling,

he takes care to enjoy the *dolce far niente* as soon as his master halts at any of the chief continental winter quarters.

The instant the carriage is unpacked, his corporeal labours cease. He then takes on himself the direction of your establishment, and sees that you are '*bien servi*,' but he will not compromise the dignity of his profession by doing anything himself. Should you drive forth from your hotel in quest of lodgings, and, in the innocence of your heart, propose to him to mount the box and give you the benefit of his experience, in making your bargain, not imagining that he can entertain any possible objection against resuming for ten minutes a seat which he has perhaps occupied daily for the last month, he will look at you as reproachfully as if you had proposed that he should deposit himself on the iron spikes behind the carriage, and will assure you that he infinitely prefers running after you on foot to the degradation of being seen accompanying your vehicle '*en ville.*'

His society is much courted by hotel keepers. Baldi of Rome keeps open house for respectable couriers out of place, in return for the custom which they have brought and may bring to them.

Your courier is a good dresser, perhaps a little over addicted to gold chains and Genoa velvet, but then that is the foreign taste.

His ostensible luggage is small, yet he sports a wonderful variety of garments; and his toilet table is crowded with an innumerable variety of brushes, bottles, and gallipots.

He generally takes lessons on the guitar and sings agreeably, talents which are duly appreciated by the lady's maid.

The poor footmen, with whom some English travellers encumber themselves, feel their inferiority, and hate him accordingly. He merely despises them.

He traffics a good deal in second-hand carriages, eau de Cologne, jewellery and gloves. He is a capital nurse in case of sickness.

To sum up the good qualities of this excellent class of servants, they are, with very few exceptions strictly honest, and grateful for any kindness shown to them; and if now and then a black sheep out of the flock should be detected levying a slight percentage on his employer's purchases, who can wonder at his so doing, when they consider with what wealthy, purse-proud, extravagant blockheads these men have often to deal?

MONACO.

EVERY morning, Sundays not excepted, a small white steamer may be seen feebly paddling out of the Port of Nice, and rounding the lighthouse of Villefranche. Her cargo generally consists of a few hampers of provisions, and of some twenty or thirty gaily-dressed people in the highest spirits. That little vessel is the *Palmaria*, the property of a well-known *industriel*, named Francis Blanc. and she is bound for the principality of Monaco, where her enterprising owner has established a gigantic gambling-house, which bids fair to rival his notorious establishment at Homburg ès Monts, near Frankfort.

At midnight, the *Palmaria* re-enters the port, and her twenty or thirty passengers, weary, soiled, sea-sick and penniless, crawl silently back to their lodgings on foot; *rouge et noir*, *roulette*, and their hotel bills seldom leaving them in a position to treat themselves to even the cheap luxury of a hackney coach.

There are two ways of reaching Monaco from Nice; one by land, the other by sea. The land journey is an affair of four hours; unless, indeed, travellers choose to ascend the Genoa road as far as Turbia, a village which stands high up on the mountain side exactly above Monaco, and to descend thence on foot by a rugged and winding mule stair to the beach below. The journey may thus be shortened nearly an hour; but the stair is steep and wearying, and is sadly trying to the feet and knees of those who are no longer young, light, and active, and who are not used to rough and broken ground.

The *Palmaria*, if the sea is smooth, and if nothing bursts or goes amiss on board, makes the passage to Monaco in an hour and a quarter; but with the slightest wind or the slightest swell she becomes abominable and dangerous. And as the calmest day may, and in the Mediterranean often does, end in a breeze towards evening, nobody who has any regard for his nose, his stomach, or his life, ought to have anything to do with that crazy little conveyance. Save and except in a dead calm she is utterly unseaworthy; and then she is generally crowded, and hot, and foul; and some of these days or nights she will either founder or drive upon the rocks, when every soul on board will perish.

Nothing can be more admirable than the scenery between Nice and Monaco, no matter whether you travel thither by land or by sea; whether you descend from Turbia on foot, or drive all the way round by Roccabruna. The only difference is, that in the one case you look down on the magnificent sight from the high mountain road, whilst in the other you look up at it from the deck of the *Palmaria*. If you go by sea, on leaving Nice, you cross the mouth of the deep harbour of Villefranche, round the rocky headland of St. Hospice—stretch across the wide bay of Beaulieu, famous for its enormous olive-trees, its bright orange-gardens, and its shady violet farms, and gaze up with wonder at the lofty grey crags of Esa and Testa di Can. In about an hour—for the *Palmaria* cannot do more than her six knots, under the most favourable circumstances—you weather Capo d'Aglio, and in ten or fifteen minutes more you are at anchor in the bay of Monaco, now the joint-property of Charles the Third of that ilk, and of Francis Blanc of Homberg ès Monts, near Frankfort.

The history of the Grimaldis, Princes of Monaco, has been intimately blended during the last eight hundred years with the histories of France, Italy, and Spain. Those who wish to acquaint themselves more minutely with its details, will do well to consult *Monaco et ses Princes, par Henri Métivier: La Flèche,* 1862—a pretentious but not uninteresting panegyric on the Grimaldi family—and a smaller and abler work, entitled, *Menton, Roquebrune, et Monaco, par Abel Rendu: Paris,* 1848.

Before carriage-roads existed, and in the infancy of gunpowder, when great ladies crossed the Alps in terror on muleback, and when battles were fought with cross-bows and matchlocks, Monaco or Mourges, the little stronghold of the Grimaldis, securely perched on its lofty rock, and commanding perfectly the sheltered haven under its guns, was necessarily a place of very considerable importance. It could only be approached in force by sea—it could only be reduced by surprise or by famine. As long as its garrison was vigilant and true, and its granaries and cisterns full, it could set the whole world at defiance. It thus constituted an admirable port of refuge for the Christian galleys of the Mediterranean—which in those contentious days constantly waged fierce war with one another and with the infidel rovers, who used sorely to harass the coasts of Italy and France, pillaging and burning the towns, carrying the inhabitants into captivity, and not unfrequently seizing and occupying for a time the strong mountain fastnesses of the *Corniche.*

The Grimaldis—at first known and dreaded as pirates—ere long assumed a foremost place amongst the great families of Italy and France, in consequence of the importance they acquired as Princes of Monaco. They allied themselves by marriage with the sovereign and royal houses of Aquitaine, Normandy, Arragon, Lorraine, Orleans, Brittany, Savoy, and Bourbon ; they distinguished themselves as soldiers and as diplomatists in almost every army and every court in Europe ; they furnished four Grand Admirals to France, several Cardinals to the Church, eleven Doges to Genoa, and a Captain-General to Florence. According to the comparative temptations and advantages held out to them, they admitted in turn within their walls, Italian, Spanish, and French garrisons, and were rewarded by Charles the Fifth and his successors, for a fidelity of more than a century, with a Grandeeship of Spain of the first class, the order of the Golden Fleece, and the grant of many valuable fiefs in the Milanese, in the kingdom of Naples, and in Spain.

But, at last, the alliance which had so long subsisted between the Giant and the Dwarf—between Madrid and Monaco—became oppressive and intolerable to the latter; and on the 13th of November, 1641, the inhabitants of the place, led by Honorius Grimaldi, surprised and expelled the Spanish force in Monaco, under Caliente. Early in the following year the Prince of Monaco visited the King of France at Peronne, and entered into a treaty with that monarch, by virtue of which his capital was thenceforward to be held by French troops, maintained and officered by France, but under the supreme command of the prince. On this occasion Louis XIII. created Honorius Duke of Valentinois and Marquis of Baux, invested him with the orders of St. Michael and of the Holy Ghost, and granted him extensive and valuable estates in France, as compensation for the dignities and revenues of which he had been deprived, in consequence of his recent rupture with Spain.

From the date of the treaty of Peronne the fortunes and the importance of Monaco appear to have gradually declined. Improvements in shipbuilding, navigation, and gunnery rendered its defences less secure, and its harbour less useful ; and its princes, having accepted the position of subjects of France, preferred residing in Paris and on their estates in Normandy, and devoting themselves entirely to the diplomacy, the arms, and the pleasures of their adopted country. During the reign of Louis XIV. the male succession to the principality of Monaco failed. Anthony the First, having no son by his wife, Mary of Lorraine, selected as the husband of his eldest daughter a French nobleman, Francis Leonor of Goyon-Matignon, Count of Thorigny, who assumed the name and arms of

Grimaldi in lieu of his own, and was created by the French King, Duke of Valentinois, during the lifetime of his father-in-law. From this marriage the present Grimaldis of Monaco are descended; so that they are, in fact, Frenchmen by blood as well as by birth and estate.

Thenceforward the Monagasques saw their princes but seldom, and seem to have been treated by them much as the Irish tenantry of the last generation used to be treated by their absentee landlords. Grasping and merciless intendants taxed them heavily and unintelligently; the monopoly of supplying the very necessaries of life was sold to foreign speculators—and the money thus painfully wrung from these simple peasants was transmitted to a distance to be squandered by sovereigns whom their subjects scarcely knew save by name. The French Revolution, therefore, found this unhappy people suffering and disaffected; they eagerly seized the opportunity of shaking off a yoke which had galled them so sorely, and quietly annexed themselves, without bloodshed, to the Great Republic.

At that time the principality consisted of the

three *communes* and towns of Monaco, Mentone, and Roccabruna, with a population of eight thousand souls subsisting on a narrow strip of rocky land at the foot of the Maritime Alps, about eight miles in length, bounded on the west by the city of Monaco and on the east by the town of Mentone. This small territory, laboriously built up into tiers of terraces, on the scanty soil of which the olive, the fig, the carob, the orange, the lemon, and the violet were cultivated, thanks to its favoured climate, with singular success, grew no corn or wine, fed neither cattle nor sheep, and was scantily supplied with water. Its inhabitants, therefore, could only subsist by exporting the luxuries, and importing the necessaries of life—a position which placed them entirely at the mercy of their administrators, who, by high duties rigorously levied, kept them in a chronic state of semi-starvation.

On the 3rd of September, 1767, a vessel carrying the Royal Standard of England entered the port of Monaco and landed the young Duke of York, brother of George III. of England, who had been taken ill at sea on his voyage from Toulon to Genoa, and claimed the hospitality of the prince. On the

14th H. R. H. expired. An autograph letter from the King is still preserved in the palace at Monaco, thanking Honorius III. for the attention and kindness which his brother had received, begging his acceptance of a set of English carriage-horses, and inviting him to London. In the spring of 1768 the prince accepted the invitation of the King of England, and some amusing memoranda exist, expressive of his Highness's delight at the attention shown to him, enumerating the exact number of guns fired in his honour when he visited Portsmouth, and dwelling especially on a certain dinner given to him by 'Milor Gramby' and General 'Couvray' at a country house called 'Inguest,' pleasantly situated on the Thames near 'Woolvich.'

In 1795, the aged Honorius died in Paris, in consequence of the long and severe imprisonment to which he had been subjected as an *aristo*. His second son, Joseph, had married in 1782, Françoise Thérése de Choiseul Stainville, and had fled with her from France on the breaking out of the Revolution, leaving their children behind them in safe hands. But the princess, unable to bear separation from her young daughters, privily returned to Paris, was discovered, seized and thrown into prison as a *suspecte*. After lingering there for some time, she was brought up before the revolutionary tribunal (7 Thermidor an II.) in company with Rouher, André Chénier, the Princess de Chimay, Baron de Trenck, M. de St. Simon, and Madame de Vigny, and was condemned to death. At that particular crisis delay was, in many cases, life, and the Princess of Monaco was advised to plead pregnancy, and to ask for a reprieve. She did so, and her plea was allowed. But it then occurred to her that, having been separated for many months from her husband, the plea she had put in was an admission of dishonour. She therefore instantly wrote to Fouquier Tinville, begging that he would visit her. Receiving no reply, she addressed to him the following letter:—

'Je vous préviens, citoyen, que je ne suis pas grosse. Je voulais vous le dire. N'espérant pas que vous viendrez, je vous le mande. Je n'ai point sali ma bouche de ce mensonge dans la crainte de la mort ni pour l'éviter, mais pour me donner un jour de plus et de couper moi-même mes cheveux, et de ne pas les donner couper de la main du bourreau. C'est le seul legs que je puisse laisser à mes enfants ; au moins faut-il qu'il soit pur.

'(Signé)

'CHOISEUL STAINVILLE JOSEPH GRIMALDI MONACO,
'*Princesse étrangère et mourante de l'injustice des juges Français.*'

On the very day on which this high-hearted and innocent woman thus wrote, she was executed. Had she remained silent but four days longer, the fall of Robespierre would have saved her.[1]

When the Allied Powers replaced Louis XVIII. on the throne of France, they restored to the Grimaldis their principality on the shore of the Mediterranean ; and towards the end of February, 1815, the Duke of Valentinois, eldest son of Honorius IV., left Paris to resume the government of Monaco on behalf of his father. At midnight, on March 1st, the duke's postchaise was stopped between Antibes and Cannes by armed men, commanded by General Cambronne. On alighting,

---

[1] See No. 2 of the *Journal de l'Opposition*, published by P. F. St. Real, in the year 3 of the Republic, p. 1. Only seven numbers of this paper appeared.

his Highness found himself in the presence of Napoleon, to whom he was intimately known, having been attached in succession to the households of the Kings of Naples and Spain, and the Empress Josephine. The Great Adventurer, who had just landed from Elba, was bivouacking in the open air by a wood-fire, amongst the olive-groves which cover that part of the coast. After a brief conversation, the two sovereigns parted, wishing each other *bonne chance*, the one for Monaco, the other for the Tuileries and St. Helena, *via* Waterloo.

By the treaty of Paris in 1815, the treaty of Peronne, which had up to that date provided that the City on the Rock should be garrisoned by French troops, was cancelled, and a fresh treaty between Piedmont and Monaco was signed at Stupiniggi in 1817, placing the King of Sardinia in the same political and military relations which the King of France had previously held with respect to the occupation of Monaco.

Adversity does not appear to have made the Grimaldis wiser or more considerate towards their subjects; they were, moreover, much poorer than they had ever been before. Taxes, therefore, were re-imposed, and monopolies of supplying bread and of coining money were re-established and sold, without regard to the interests or the capabilities of the taxed to bear the burdens thus capriciously and mercilessly heaped upon them. At last, after frequent and unheeded expostulations, Roccabruna and Mentone, unable to endure any longer the misgovernment to which they were subjected, rose in 1847, and driving out the representatives of the Grimaldis, proclaimed themselves free towns, and claimed and obtained as such the protection of Piedmont ;—the city of Monaco and the morsel of territory immediately around it, chiefly in the hands of retainers and servants of the Prince and of State officials, alone remaining faithful to its sovereign.

In this unsettled and disjointed position the affairs of the Grimaldi family remained until 1859 ; and when, after the peace of Villafranca, Nice and Savoy were ceded by Italy to France, a new arrangement was entered into with respect to the revolted *communes* of the Prince of Monaco. The Emperor of the French agreed to pay to Charles III.

four millions of francs, in consideration of the formal cession of his claims, and Roccabruna and Mentone were annexed to France, whose frontier on the sea-shore was thus extended as far as the bridge of St. Louis—a mile to the eastward of Mentone.

The present Prince of Monaco, therefore, only now retains sovereignty over his ancient capital, and over about a square mile of stony olive-grounds and orange and lemon gardens around it—his subjects do not number 1,000 souls, his standing army consists of but twelve privates, two non-commissioned officers, and a drummer; and his dominions are protected on three sides by French custom-house officers, and on the fourth by the blue waters of the Mediterranean.

And it is with this illustrious Italian prince—the only one whose hereditary rights have escaped the consolidating tendency which has welded together the other small states of the peninsula into the great and powerful kingdom of Italy—it is with the representative of the old and famous family of Grimaldi that M. François Blanc, of Homburg ès Monts, near Frankfort, has entered into a pecuniary arrangement for the abuse of his ancestral domain for purposes of *roulette* and *rouge et noir!*

M. Blanc and his shareholders are wise in their generation. The leaders of the German Confederation have of late, on more occasions than one, exhibited manifest signs of impatience at the discredit which is brought upon their order by the cupidity of certain princes, who for a consideration have been willing to sell toleration and indulgences to 'the professors of the speculative sciences,' as the gamblers of the Rhine euphuistically call themselves. M. Benazet, at Baden, has already received notice to quit, and it is more than probable that during the next political *remue-ménage* which convulses Germany, Spa, Ems, Wiesbaden, Homburg, and Nauheim will summarily purge themselves of the harpies who infest and fatten upon their visitors, by the brisk Transatlantic process familiarly known as 'Lynch law.' In anticipation of some such catastrophe, the venerable M. Blanc has pitched upon Monaco as a secure haven of refuge for his declining years, and it must be admitted that he has made a most judicious selection. With a delicious climate, sheltered in winter from the prevailing winds, its proximity to the mountains and the sea, and the dense shade of its prodigious olive-groves, make it cool and pleasant in summer; its scenery is unrivalled, even along the celebrated *Corniche*; and the shelving nature of its shore, and its delicate sands and smooth black rocks, render the sea-bathing at Monaco perfect. In a very short time the railroad from Nice to Genoa will daily bring abundant grist to M. Blanc's money-mills from all parts of France and Italy, and the horrors and dangers of the abominable little *Palmaria*, and the pains and penalties of the steep and stony mule-stair between Monaco and Turbia, will become matters of ancient history.

The *Palmaria* comes to an anchor below the City on the Rock about noon; and boats in the pay of M. Blanc land her passengers, who are immediately hurried off in omnibuses and carriages— also in the pay of M. Blanc—to his Casino, which stands above the eastern side of the harbour— nearly a mile from the landing-place and the city. The aspect of Monaco from the sea almost baffles the power of words to describe it as it deserves to be described. It covers the whole of a small table-shaped rock of reddish hue, rising a couple of hundred feet sheer out of the sea, and projecting from the foot of the lofty mountain, on the top of which frowns the grim grey crag known as the Testa di Can. This little peninsula is wrought over with picturesque and complicated fortifications—impregnable 150 years ago—contemptible enough now. Behind them are to be seen the white houses and churches of the old city, its huge barrack, recently converted into a refuge for Jesuits, and its enormous palace. Intermixed with its buildings are numerous gardens and public walks, adorned with tall parasol pines, dark cypress and ilex, graceful palms, fantastic fig-trees, and bright orange-trees; the decaying masonry of its walls and the rock itself being covered with a riotous growth of wild geranium, myrtle, oleander, aloes, euphorbia, cactus, and Indian fig. A carriage-road has been contrived from the beach to the city, by the sacrifice of a portion of its useless fortifications; before this new road was made the only access to Monaco was by a steep paved mule-stair—similar to that which connects it with Turbia.

There is not much to be seen within its walls,

save the views—which are magnificent on all sides. Its palace, stripped and dismantled during the French Revolution—afterwards served as a hospital for sick and wounded soldiers during Napoleon's Italian campaigns—and was used from 1806 to 1814 as a *dépôt de Mendicité* for the departments of the Maritime Alps. For upwards of a quarter of a century afterwards it remained in a neglected and dilapidated condition; but in 1841 some repairs were made to it by Florestan I., and by the reigning Prince it has been entirely restored and refurnished. It is not at present shown to the public —nor does it contain any pictures, statues, or objects of *vertu*, worthy the attention of the connoisseur. Its gardens, however, are said to be very beautiful and curious.

In front of the palace is a wide parade-ground shaded by ancient plane-trees, under which peacefully repose forty huge brass cannon—dismounted —the gift of Louis XIV. to his faithful ally. Four streets connected by transverse lanes lead from the parade-ground to the *Promenade de St. Martin* at the other end of the city, and when the visitor has inspected them, walked round the ramparts and looked into a pretty public garden, called, *Le Desert*, he has seen nearly all that is worth seeing in Monaco.

Descending to the port, the road passes by an extensive bathing establishment, constructed in the bight of the little bay, and much resorted to by visitors during the spring and summer months, and leaving the rich orange-gardens of *La Condamine* on its left, climbs abruptly up the face of the rock on the eastern side of the harbour to the *Plateau des Spelugues*—which, being interpreted from the Monagasque patois—means the Plain of the Robbers. And it is on this spot that M. Blanc of Homburg ès Monts, near Frankfort, has established himself and his gambling-tables.

To give that enterprising individual his due— he is a very clever fellow, and does things grandly and in excellent taste. All that the most lavish expenditure and the most skilful landscape-gardening and architecture can do, has been done, and is doing, to enhance, if possible, the natural beauties of this charming site. Several acres in the centre of the plateau have been cleared of the enormous olive-trees by which it is covered, and a handsome

Grecian edifice overlooking the sea, and commanding an extensive view on all sides, has been recently completed.

The ceremony of laying the first stone of the *Elysium Alberti*, as it was called in 1858, was made an affair of state, at which the heir apparent—Prince Albert, an interesting child of ten years old—was permitted to preside; and in the same year his father instituted a new order of knighthood, that of St. Charles of Monaco, with regard to which the court historian, Henri Métivier, writes, 'Le port de cette décoration, accordé avec une sage reserve, a été autorisé en France, en Espagne, en Italie, en Suède, et dans divers États de l'Allemagne.'

The falling ground in front of the Casino has been arranged in a succession of architectural terraces, planted with ornamental shrubs and flowers; and low down on the beach below, the railroad from Nice to Genoa is to pass. Behind the Casino a large square has been laid out, the western side of which is occupied by the *Grand Hôtel de Paris*, and the eastern by a spacious range of stabling, masked under the guise of a Swiss *châlet.* Several newly-erected villas are already completed, and on all sides venerable and decrepit olive-trees, hundreds of years old, are falling to the woodman's axe, to make room for the operations of the builder.

The interior of the Casino presents the scene familiar to *habitués* of German watering places. At the doors visitors are received by the usual tall, grave men, half servants, half *mouchards*, clad in M. Blanc's well-known blue and red liveries, laced with gold, and wearing the normal drab gaiters. In the ball-room are the usual marble columns, gilded ceiling, and *parqueté* floor, and the usual band of twenty-four performers executing the usual opera tunes. On one side of the ball-room is the *salon de lecture*, well supplied with papers and periodicals, and on the other M. Blanc's workshop, the *salon de jeu*. As yet there does not seem to be very much doing there, and M. Blanc's daily expenditure must be enormous. The *Grand Hôtel de Paris* is, however, always full. The *Palmaria* brings from Nice a couple of cargoes every day, wind and weather permitting, and takes back the empty bottles; and, in a week or two, a better and larger steamer—which will not be difficult to find—is to be placed on the station. Then there is an omnibus constantly plying to and fro between Nice and Monaco, by the high mountain road; and there are also numerous visitors who arrive daily in hired carriages, or who walk down from Turbia. And as nobody ever seems to win, it is calculated that, even now, M. Blanc makes both ends meet, and something more; and when the railway opens his prospects will be prodigious. Mysterious young couples—handsome, well-dressed, and *bien gantés*—who are always described by the waiters as distinguished members of the Jockey Club and celebrated actresses from Paris, saunter superciliously about the walks, dine expensively by themselves in the *restaurant*, play heavily for a time, and then disappear; raffish middle-aged Englishmen looking as if they had seen better days, and were very likely to see worse, infest the *table d'hôte*, criticise the cook, patronise the waiters, and profess to be detained for letters which never seem to arrive; and a variety of young ladies wearing pork-pie hats, rumpled and touzled hair, and high-heeled, long-quartered shoes, scurry about the gardens and saloons in loose gaudy dresses, smoking cigarettes, chatting familiarly with the *employés*, and appearing to belong to nobody in particular. Who they are, how they live, or what they are doing at Monaco, Charles III. and M. Blanc alone can tell. If the RR. PP. S. J. have to look after the morals of these mysterious damsels, the task must be one well calculated to call forth all the energy and talent which distinguish that vigorous but unappreciated order of religionists, and satisfactorily accounts for their sudden appearance in such force at Monaco.

Roulette is as yet the popular game, which is a sure sign that there is no serious play going on. The dealers at the *rouge-et-noir* board apparently go through their operations from habit and from a sense of duty, rather than for any practical object, so trifling are the stakes, and so obvious is it that the bearded and decorated individuals who pretend to risk them, and whose red ribands, it is to be hoped, indicate the *Grand Cordon* of the order of St. Charles, are mere 'bonnets.' But as, at his Monaco *roulette* table, M. Blanc prudently reserves to himself the substantial perquisite of two zeros, being well content at Homburg with but one, it is not very difficult to guess how it comes to pass that the return passengers by the *Palmaria* almost always have to walk home from the port on foot.[1]

The *Grand Hôtel de Paris* is in all respects excellent, and by no means unreasonably dear, considering that nothing save oranges, lemons, oil, and dried violets is produced or sold at Monaco, and that everything else must be brought from abroad. All M. Blanc's *employés*, as well as the sirens in the pork-pie hats, reside in the old city on the opposite side of the bay—there being no accommodation for them as yet on the Plain of the Robbers. Omnibuses drawn by four horses ply *gratis* for their convenience several times a day between the Casino and the Rock, where the society must be of a curiously mixed description, to judge from the recent liberal importations of Jesuits, musicians, lorettes, and gamblers which the firm of Grimaldi and Blanc have made. It is unpleasant to think upon the effects of this unholy invasion on the future of the little community, and to reflect that

---

[1] *Roulette* is now played at Monaco with one zero, and *rouge-et noir* with the half *réfait*.—January, 1866.

it has been brought about solely in order that the last of the reigning princes of Italy and a French hell-keeper may 'make their game' to advantage, and set the police regulations of both countries at defiance, at the expense of the travelling public.

From the *Plateau des Spelugues* a very pretty road runs along the coast through the celebrated lemon-gardens of the old principality as far as Roccabruna, where it joins the main road from Nice to Genoa. The *citronniers* of Monaco supply a most valuable article of export, their fruit having the reputation of keeping longer and bearing voyages better than the lemons of any other district of Italy. The three *communes* have, in good seasons, exported as many as thirty millions of them.

The *Journal de Monaco*, the organ of the Palace and the Casino, is published once a week by A. Chambon, 18, Rue de Lorraine. It issues the official notices of the Government, which seem to refer chiefly to the appointment of vice-consuls abroad, and to the distribution of the Order of St.

Charles of Monaco. It chronicles the dinners, receptions, concerts, and balls given by Charles III. and by M. Blanc, and generally on alternate Sundays devotes a *premier*-Monaco to the praise of one of that gentleman's two gambling-houses. Although it announces every week that both Monagasque and foreign authors may have their writings reviewed in its columns on forwarding two copies of their works, post paid, to the editor, it would seem that this liberal offer has not hitherto been appreciated by the *littérateurs* of Europe, for no reviews ever appear in it; and its advertisements are generally limited to the hours of the arrival and departure of the *Palmaria* and the omnibus.

On November 1, 1863, the *Journal* announced that the Prince of Monaco had very appropriately bestowed upon George I., King of the Greeks, the Grand Cordon of the Order of St. Charles.

Its commercial intelligence is characteristic :—

'Il s'est fait cette semaine passée quelques affaires sur les oranges. On en a vendu un lot de 50,000 à raison de 10 francs le mille. Les affaires sur les citrons et sur les huiles ont été calmes.

'Le prix des citrons s'est considérablement élevé depuis ces derniers froids. Il y a un mois à peine ils ne valaient pas 10 francs par mille; aujourd'hui les marchands étrangers viennent faire des offres beaucoup plus élevés. Ils ont voulu prendre à 20 francs. Les détenteurs ont refusé de vendre. On compte sur une reprise plus forte. Quelques propriétaires ne désespèrent pas de les voir à 40 francs avant la fin du mois.'

From time immemorial a sort of *tableau vivant*, representing the Passion and Crucifixion of our Saviour, used to be enacted in the streets of Monaco on Good Friday. Abel Rendu gives the following graphic description of it :—

'As the clock strikes nine, the city, illuminated, bursts into a blaze of light, and the chapel of the palace is seen, decorated as if for a festival. A tribune and his guards, helmet on head and lance in hand, open the procession. Christ, represented by a dignified inhabitant of the principality, follows in deep affliction, his eyes suffused with tears. The treacherous Judas approaches his master, and betrays him to his followers, who bind his hands, scourge him with rods, and throw over him in mockery the purple robe. Herod, prouder of his absurd parasol than a pacha of his three tails, Peter, brandishing his sword, Malchus, with his bleeding ear, the chief priests and elders clamouring for our Saviour's blood, Pilate washing his hands, the soldiers casting lots for the garments of Christ, and the executioner preparing himself for his cruel office, all appear in succession. Then Jesus, pale and sinking, is laden with his heavy cross, he is nailed to it, and soon gives up the ghost.

'The accusing cock, the cries of death, the sponge dipped in gall, the sharp lance, the weeping Magdalen, St. John and his lamb—are all represented; but that is not enough—the tragedy soon merges into a farce.

'A group difficult to describe unexpectedly presents itself—it consists of our First Parents, of the Tempter, and of the Angel with the flaming sword. Then comes Judith and her maid, St. Lawrence and his gridiron, St. Philomene and her anchor, and after them the Twelve Apostles carrying the various instruments of their martyrdom. In the midst floats the banner of Rome. All these notabilities, resuscitated for the occasion, hasten to assist at the solemn inhumation of Christ.

'The body of the Saviour is carried along on a bier, covered by a dais, and surrounded by torchbearers. The drums beat. The holy women weep. The people mutter prayers as the procession enters the chapel and escorts the Victim to his tomb. A sermon on the Passion concludes the strange exhibition—solemn and impressive to the actors—grotesque and unedifying in the eyes of strangers.'

About the year 1848 the Bishop of Nice, shocked at the profanity of the show, forbade its repetition, and for some years it remained in abeyance. But under the auspices of the enterprising M. Blanc the Sacred Mystery has been revived, improved, and utilised, and the *Journal de Monaco* of March 27, 1864, announced that on Good Friday last entirely new dresses, decorations, and accessories of a magnificent and ingenious character had been provided for it at the expense of the *Société Anonyme des Jeux*, which also liberally imported for the occasion a brass band, and chartered a steamboat capable of conveying eight hundred pilgrims from Nice to the Rock, on the sagacious calculation that many of the strangers who came to scoff would remain to play. The description given by the *Journal de Monaco* of the evening's amusement tallies pretty nearly with that given by Abel Rendu sixteen years ago, with the exception that, on this last occasion, a large appletree was borne before Adam and Eve, from which our First Parents plucked apples, and cast them to be scrambled for by the surrounding crowd as the procession moved on.

A DAY WITH THE EMPEROR'S HOUNDS.

THERE is probably no human being more dogmatical than your thorough British sportsman. He firmly believes that but one correct and orthodox system of dealing with the *feræ naturæ* exists, and that is the traditional system which has been practised time out of mind by his own countrymen. He cannot persuade himself that 'Frenchmen'—in which comprehensive denomination he conveniently includes all mankind who do not happen to be British subjects—can either ride, shoot, hunt, or fish, save after the abortive and unsatisfactory methods peculiar to 'tailors' and 'muffs.' A 'foreigner's' account of a day's sport of any kind convulses him with contemptuous laughter, for he at once detects in it a thousand unimportant flaws and blemishes which confirm him in his creed, that 'Frenchmen' are pre-ordained by nature to be, and to remain, ignorant all their lives of everything which a thorough British sportsman ought instinctively to know. 'How, indeed,' will he ask, 'is it possible to listen gravely to a fellow who talks of "a covey" of snipe, "a couple" of partridges, or "the tail" 'of a fox?'

I confess that I am not without serious misgivings that this intolerant spirit may not be confined to British sportsmen, but that it may equally prevail amongst the sportsmen of other nations; that American back-woodsmen may very possibly hold the solemn English swells who write pretentious books about buffalo hunting quite as cheap as we hold 'foreigners' in general, in all matters pertaining to English wood-craft; and that a Gaucho rough-rider may, on his own ground, justly consider himself a better man across country than the best of our Leicestershire chivalry, if, indeed, the Gaucho has ever heard of the existence of those gentlemen.

It is, therefore, with some diffidence that I proceed, at the instigation of my friends, Messrs. Smith and Elder, to jot down on paper my recollections of a day's stag hunting, which it was once my good fortune to see with the French Emperor's hounds in the forest of Compiègne. I must premise by stating that I know nothing of the noble science of venery as practised by the high school of French sportsmen; that I knew next to nothing of the localities in which the hunt I am about to describe took place, and that I knew scarcely any of the sportsmen or women who were present at it, even by sight. I fear, therefore, that this paper may appear as entirely and hopelessly absurd in the eyes of the members of the Imperial Hunt as would, to the readers of *Bell's Life* or the *Field*, a narrative by one of Mr. Leech's most egregious hunting 'mossoos' of 'a clipping thing with the Queen's,' from Ivor Heath or Salt Hill.

Stag hunting, as practised in the immediate neighbourhood of London, cannot, I imagine, be considered, even by its most enthusiastic votaries, as a very elevated branch of the wild sports of Middlesex. You do not, indeed, hunt a wild animal at all; you hunt a wretched tame brute, kept up in a stable, fed upon the best of beans, oats, and old hay, and chased round a paddock daily for the improvement of its wind and condition. You convey it to the place of execution in a van drawn by post-horses; you flavour it highly with aniseed in order to solve all doubts and difficulties as to scent; as the clock strikes eleven you 'enlarge' it, and 'chivy' it furiously for half a mile with horsewhips and execrations 'to give it a start,' and you then lay on your hounds.

As the poor beast generally prefers running along the roads,—if the weather is dry and the roads hard,—its feet soon give way and it is easily taken; but if the roads chance to be soft, or if it betakes itself, as it sometimes will, to the ploughed lands, the chase is longer, and usually ends in some pond or stream, into which the hot and wearied deer rushes when it is utterly blown. Occasionally, the hounds maul and mangle it so badly before the huntsmen can ride up to save it, that it has to be killed then and there, for as its horns are sawn off, it has no means of defending itself; oftener, however, it is secured by the aid of hunting whips and ropes, and is hauled into the nearest barn or coach-house, where it remains a prisoner until its van arrives to convey it home again. A few weeks' nursing qualifies it to appear in public once more, and so its miserable life passes away, until some sad day its feet are entirely destroyed by the Macadam, or the hounds, distancing the huntsmen, tear it to pieces. Between the fate of a badger, kept in a box to be 'drawn,' and that of a deer kept in a paddock to be hunted, there is, in fact, very little to choose.

I have prefixed this bald sketch of our method of hunting the tame deer in Middlesex to the present paper in order to bespeak from my English readers some indulgence—if they discover during the course of my narrative that the sportsmen of France, in finding, hunting, and killing the wild stag, in its native forest, do not carry on their operations precisely in the same way as Mr. Davis, the Queen's huntsman, does. *Tot homines quot sententiæ.* There is, doubtless, a good deal to be said in favour of both systems; yet I am convinced that, were I a stag, I should approve of neither, and should denounce them as equally cruel and unfair.

On a fine sharp November morning, in the year 1862, I left Paris by the Northern Railway at 9 A.M., having sent on my horses the day before to the *Hôtel de la Cloche*, at Compiègne, in order

A Day with the Emperor's Hounds. 199

to have a day with the Emperor's hounds. I knew nobody connected with the Court, nor did I even know whether I had any business, as a stranger, to join the Imperial Hunt at all. Nevertheless, I had heard so much of the beauty of the forest, and the splendour of the pageant, that I determined to take my chance as to the reception which an uninvited and unknown stranger would receive from the *Grand Veneur*.

The journey to Compiègne was accomplished in about an hour and a half. In the carriage with me were several gentlemen wearing the livery of the Hunt—a very neat and becoming dress. It consists of a small tricorn hat, a loose dark green cutaway coat, and a red waistcoat, all richly bound and braided with gold, white leather breeches, Napoleon boots, and a *couteau de chasse*. An omnibus conveyed us across the river Oise and up the steep streets of the town to the *Hôtel de la Cloche*, where we found breakfast prepared for us. The inn stables were crowded with grooms and hunters awaiting their masters from Paris, and two or three very light open carriages, kept for the purpose, drawn by white post-horses, were ready to convey to the meet several other parties, who, like myself, had come to see the show. One of the first persons I stumbled across was a stableman I recollected to have seen in the service of Mr. Z., the well-known London horse-dealer. I asked him what he was doing at Compiègne. 'Brought over a couple of hosses, sir, for Miss ——, to sell to the Hemperor;' and, sure enough, there was that accomplished little heart- and horse- breaker attired in one of Poole's neatest riding-habits, standing smiling at my elbow, booted and spurred, and eager for the fray.

As soon as I could find my servant and horses, I mounted, and rode slowly on towards the meet. The forest commences the moment you leave the town. It covers 30,000 acres of ground, contains several large pieces of water, and is bounded on its western side by the Oise. Its soil appeared to me to be green sand upon clay; it rode quite as clean and sound as the Nottinghamshire dukeries ride, and it grows finer oaks than either Clumber, Welbeck, or Worksop can boast. It is pierced in all directions by no less than 1,100 *kilomètres* of wide, well-kept rides; and, at intervals of about two miles, are open spaces called *carrefours de chasse*, about as big as Berkeley Square, from each of which these rides diverge in eight different directions. Innumerable guide-posts direct the stranger through what would be a hopeless labyrinth without them.

The meet on the occasion of which I am writing was the *Carrefour du Puits du Roi*, six miles from Compiègne.

On entering the forest I overtook the hounds, upwards of thirty couples of large, strong, and rather coarse dogs. They were attended by four *valets de chiens*, on foot, and by two *piqueurs*, riding handsome English horses. These servants were dressed in the Imperial livery, and carried around them French horns, the footmen wearing long white stockings gartered with black garters below their knees, and high-low shoes; with their tricorn hats they looked very much like Knaves of Spades. They were short, sturdy fellows, and during the day they had plenty of opportunities of showing that they knew their craft right well, and were gifted with wonderful speed and bottom. A portion of the hounds had soft white cords coiled round their necks, raising, in the minds of the uninitiated, doubts whether they were going to hunt or going to be hanged. But it was explained to me, that it is the custom with French stag hunters to station in various parts of the forest *relais*, consisting of two or three couples of hounds, in charge of a *valet*, in order that they may be *lancés* on the stag if he happens to come near them, and that these cords were required to lead the *relais* to their posts, and to restrain them till the moment arrived for slipping them.

In company with the hounds we jogged on, passing alternately under lofty timber and by low copse, along firm sandy rides until we reached the *Carrefour du Puits du Roi.* We there found eight *gendarmes* in full uniform, mounted on tall bay Norman horses, one being posted at each of the eight entrances to the *carrefour.* At two or three small stalls women were selling coffee, brandy, bread, and roasted chestnuts; a large wood fire was blazing and crackling away merrily, sending its tall column of grey smoke up amongst the trees by which our place of *rendezvous* was overshadowed, and half-a-dozen light carriages filled with ladies were drawn up on the edge of the wood, so as to leave the space within the *carrefour* quite free. The hounds grouped themselves on the green sward around the Knaves of Spades who had them in charge; and we all betook ourselves to drinking coffee and burning *gloria*, and munching bread and chestnuts, and smoking—and waited.

Presently we espied, far away down one of the green rides, a troop of horsemen slowly approaching. As it closed up, we discovered it to consist of fifty prime English hunters, covered with green and gold clothing, marked with the Imperial crown and *chiffre*, and ridden and led by twenty-five neat grooms in the Imperial liveries. Five or six of the horses bore ladies' saddles. This cavalcade entered the *carrefour* and drew up in line on the side opposite to that on which the hounds were rolling, gamboling, and fighting. Then there was another very long pause, only broken by the occasional arrival of a *calèche* and posters, or of a gentleman in the livery of the Hunt. At last a prodigious cracking of whips and jingling of bells announced that the *cortége* from the Castle was at hand. And exactly at 1 P. M. ten *chars à bancs* dashed into the *carrefour*, preceded by the *Grand Veneur* on horseback. Each *char à bancs* carried twelve persons, sitting, three abreast, on four seats, and was drawn by six horses and attended by two mounted *piqueurs*. The horses were all bay Percheron mares about 15.3 in height, handsome, round, and strong, and very fast trotters; their manes were plaited, their tails clubbed, their rope traces preposterously long, their small neat heads abundantly garnished with bells and badger fur. The postilions and *piqueurs* all wore round glazed hats, powder, pigtails, green and gold jackets, and red waistcoats, leather breeches, and heavy jack-boots, after the fashion of the olden time, and wielded their whips with deafening dexterity.

The Emperor did not hunt on this occasion, having to attend a Council of State. But in the front seat of the first *char à bancs* sat the Empress and the Princess Anna Murat, with a gentleman whose name I could not learn. These two ladies also wore the livery of the Hunt, less—of course—the breeches, boots, and *couteaux de chasse*, the Empress's tricorn having the distinctive ornament of a white ostrich feather coiled around its crown. Amongst the company in the *chars à bancs* I recognised a couple of English dukes, and some half dozen other English personages of note. Horses

A Day with the Emperor's Hounds. 205

were provided for everybody who chose to ride, and several of the English visitors availed themselves of the Emperor's liberality in this respect, but the greater portion of the party from the Castle appeared to prefer following the hunt on wheels.

As soon as the Empress and Princess Murat had mounted, the *Grand Veneur* informed her Majesty that two stags had been rounded up in the early morning by the keepers and their *limiers*, and were known to be within a short distance of the meet. The Empress at once indicated the direction in which she preferred that the sport should commence, and cantered off with her party, followed by about forty gentlemen wearing the livery of the Hunt, the Imperial *chars à bancs*, a few officers in uniform belonging to the *Chasseurs d'Afrique* in garrison at Compiègne, a good many *gendarmes* who perform the police of the forest, and a perfect cloud of *piqueurs* and grooms. Myself and a little niece of mine, who had accompanied me on her pony, were the only two 'civilians' present on horseback, save and except the pretty little horse-dealing horse-breaker; and the very strong doubts which I entertained whether we might not be looked upon as intruders induced me to keep aloof from the Imperial party, and to ride within the margin of the forest.

On reaching the next *carrefour*, we learned that the stag, disturbed by the noise of the approaching throng, was already afoot, and had just crossed it. A sort of semicircle was therefore formed, of which the Empress was the centre, and the hounds were brought by their *valets* to be laid on the scent. Before this ceremony took place, my little niece said to me, 'I am sure that the Empress is looking at us. See, she is sending that gentleman to tell us to go away,' and, sure enough, at that very moment an *aide-de-camp*, who had been speaking to her Majesty, hat in hand, suddenly turned his horse round, and galloped straight up to the spot where we were standing. I was preparing to apologise for my intrusion, and to beat a retreat with the best grace I could, when the 'Frenchman' courteously addressed us, saying, 'The Empress requests that the young English lady on the piebald pony will ride up to her side, where she will see the sport much better than where she is now placed;' and accordingly the young English lady, who was but fourteen years old, did canter up to where the

Empress of the French stood, and rode by the side of that kind lady during a great portion of the day. When she is at home, in England, she lives in a midland county, near one of the exiled princes of the House of Orleans, who is as popular with his neighbours as such a courteous, manly, and intelligent gentleman deserves to be; and until her memorable ride in the forest of Compiègne, I am convinced that my little niece May was one of the most devoted adherents the Orleans dynasty had; but such is the frailty and corruption of the female heart, that from that day forward her views on French politics have undergone an entire change. She has, I lament to say, been ever since a rank Imperialist, and I doubt whether even Mr. Kinglake's celebrated fourteenth chapter would succeed in inducing the grateful and proud little girl to think any ill of the terrible Man of December, whose beautiful and gentle wife was so thoughtful and good-natured to her, a child and a stranger, during their pleasant gallop through the forest of Compiègne on that bright November morning. It seems so easy for royalty to win popularity by small courtesies like these, that I often wonder why the attempt is so seldom made. I never saw it made before, yet I can answer for it that on this occasion it succeeded perfectly.

As soon as the hounds were away, the sport proceeded as prosperously as woodland hunting on a good scenting day generally does. We galloped up one ride and down another, guided chiefly by the *cors de chasse* of the huntsmen, which made known to the initiated the direction in which the stag was tending. At one time he was declared to be making straight for the *Etangs de St. Pierre*, at another for the *Grands Réservoirs*, and we varied our course accordingly. At last, after running within the forest for upwards of an hour and a half, he broke cover, crossed a strip of cultivated land about a mile in width, and plunged into the Oise, followed by the hounds. In an incredibly short time all the huntsmen, horse and foot, were collected on the bank of the river, encouraging the hounds with their voices and their horns; and they were soon joined by the Empress and her party. The *chars à bancs*, which had followed the chase with great spirit and success as long as the stag remained in cover, were here thrown out, not being able to get across the deep ploughed land, and came to a halt in the high road which runs between the forest and the river.

At this moment a curious little episode in the day's sport occurred. A light *calèche* drove noisily up, drawn by four of the Imperial-horses, and out of it two ladies handed the *Prince Impérial*, a sturdy comely boy of seven years old, with chubby cheeks and crisp curling black hair. He, too, was dressed in the livery of his father's Hunt, wearing a little tricorn hat with an ostrich feather, a little green cut-away coat, and a little red waistcoat laced with gold, little white leather breeches, and little Napoleon boots, and I am obliged to confess that he looked extremely like General Tom Thumb. A mite of a pony, as narrow as a penknife, was in waiting for him. He mounted it with great confidence, and proceeded to canter boldly and easily across the ploughed field to the river side to join his mother and witness the death of the stag. His governor rode by his side, two grooms followed, and four *gendarmes* watchfully prevented the crowd from pressing too close upon his heels.

The sight, when we reached the river, was very

striking. Under the bank were grouped the *valets de chiens* and the huntsmen in a high state of excitement; above it stood the Empress, the *Prince Impérial*, and their *suite*, and on the opposite side of the Oise were about a hundred men in blue blouses—the inhabitants of a neighbouring village, who had turned out to see the fun. Behind us were the tall dark timber trees of the forest, in front, a wide, open, cultivated plain, and high upon our left, the town and castle of Compiègne, distant about five miles. The stag was swimming about at his ease in the river, the hounds seemed much distressed, and a couple of huntsmen in a punt, with short carbines, were endeavouring to get into a position from which they could shoot the animal without danger to the hounds or to the people on the banks. After a good deal of dodging and one or two misses, a lucky shot struck it in the neck, when it turned short round, met the hounds, and was almost instantly drowned by them.

The day's sport was then over, and we devoted our best energies to getting back to Compiègne as fast and as fussily as we could. Why we were in such a hurry I cannot say. A wonderfully well appointed *calèche* awaited the Empress in the high road, and trotted off with her and Princess Anna Murat; another, in which the *Prince Impérial's* governess and *bonne* were waiting for him, reconveyed that precocious young potentate back to his nursery; the *chars à bancs* followed in their wake, as did the sportsmen and women on horseback and the crowd of grooms and *piqueurs*, the hounds remaining in charge of the footmen. Such a brilliant scramble and scurry I never before witnessed, such cracking of whips and jingling of bells and trotting of horses; the stout Percheron mares, in spite of the unsparing way in which they had been 'bucketed' up and down the forest rides for several hours, taking home their heavy *chars à bancs* with the greatest ease at the rate of eleven miles an hour.

At the *Cloche*, at Compiègne, a *table d'hôte* was ready for us hungry hunters as soon as we arrived. Overtures were made to me during the evening for the purchase both of my own horse and my niece's pony on such tempting terms that I found it very difficult to resist them; a corpulent capitalist, who had passed the day lazily in one of the Imperial *chars à bancs*, sending me word that he would give any price in reason for '*le merveilleux cob*' which the tall Englishman had ridden—the said cob being sixteen hands high and eighteen years old! We were told that we ought to repair at nine o'clock to the courtyard of the castle, where the *curée*, or breaking up of the stag, would take place by torch-light, in presence of the Emperor and the Court. But at nine o'clock the last train started for Paris—so the *curée* we could not and did not see. But my groom—a grumbling Englishman—who hated being away from his wife and his beer, and who voted Paris 'a poor place,' and declared that English horses must inevitably become broken-winded if they eat French hay—did see it, and told me, to my surprise, that it was such a 'stunning' sight that he would have walked all the way from England rather than have missed it. Being a man of few words, he would not or could not explain to me what there was in the ceremony which struck his torpid fancy so much, but such was Jack Raven's report of the *curée* by torchlight at Compiègne, and I give it for what it may be worth.

At the railway station we entered an empty carriage, from which we were speedily ejected by the station-master, who told us that it was specially reserved for a great lady from the Castle, and, presently, the pretty little horsebreaker, who had been had over 'special' from London to exhibit and sell Mr. Z.'s horses to the Emperor, but who had failed in her mission in consequence of his Majesty's absence on affairs of state, was ceremoniously handed into it by the Emperor's head groom, the guard blew his horn—the train started—we all fell asleep—and by half-past ten we were drinking tea and talking over our day's sport in our apartments at the *Grand Hôtel du Louvre*.

REFORM YOUR WALTZING.

A NEAT little book was put forward under the above title a couple of years ago by Messrs. Longman. A second edition is, we understand, in the press, with a supplement containing Meditations on the Polka, by a Bavarian diplomatist, and the Physiology of the Cellarius by the distinguished professor who invented and gave his name to that graceful dance.

The author takes for his text the dictum that 'waltzing is the art of a gentleman, and never yet was taught or understood by a dancing-master.'

To an unlearned eye the diagrams and directions by which he asserts his claim to gentility appear hopelessly abstruse and complicated; and although a practised dancer may possibly find little difficulty in unravelling them, yet as we presume that the object of an amateur is rather to instruct the ignorant than to address the adroit, we must entreat that he will not cast aside his pen until he has given us clearer and ampler directions on a topic which, in the present day, interests so deeply the head of every family.

His view of waltzing as practised in Britain is gloomy in the extreme. He deplores the clumsiness of the English as a nation, and even ventures to affirm that 'he never has yet met with two persons together who did the real three steps backward and forward of the Rhenish waltz in the perfection of which it is susceptible.'

Now this is really going too far. We maintain, in despite of the amateur's assertions, that London, during the season, contains some of the finest waltzers, both indigenous and exotic, that the civilised world has generated.

We would back ourselves, with the aid of the court newsman, to bring to bear at a very few hours' notice on any given point where the champagne was good and the plovers' eggs genuine, scores of elegant young men unsurpassable in speed, endurance and oiliness of incession. The government offices, the foot-guards, and the Local Horse, are a host in themselves, not to mention the agile and energetic *attachés* to the various foreign missions at our court.

Moreover, it is well known that a large and well-organised body of young men exists in London, under the conduct of the ubiquitous Alphonse Tiptoe, who earn their daily bread solely by their proficiency in the Waltz, Polka, and Cellarius.

We do not publish this fact to their disadvantage. Far from it. For how, we pause to enquire, can a man earn his livelihood more creditably than by the sweat of his brow?

These deserving and hard-working votaries of Terpsichore are well-made, active fellows, tastily but inexpensively dressed, who would be equally well calculated for the vocation of lamplighters, or for any other calling which depended more upon their calves than their brains. Indeed, it has been intimated to us, that when the London season is over, those members of the Dancing Club who do not travel about the country professionally with Weippert and Jullien, or betake themselves to Paris, *pour raviver leur Polka*, endeavour to keep up their condition, and earn a few shillings by feats of pedestrianism in the suburbs of London, which are recorded in *Bell's Life*, as those of the Piccadilly Pet, the Belgravian Snob, the Mayfair Deer, &c.

From February to August they are diffused throughout the ball-rooms of London wherever link-boys and fiddles are to be heard and lobster-salads to be eaten, in Baker Street and in Belgravia, at the Lord Mayor's ball and at Devonshire House, dancing indiscriminately with everything female, *qui leur vient sous la main*, for it is the grand principle of their profession to be impartial.

They give themselves no airs, are civil to every one, venerate ball-rooms much, and dinner-givers more, and acquire marvellous adroitness in discovering mislaid shawls, getting up family coaches in a crowd, and transporting corpulent *chaperons* from place to place with celerity and precision. They are not much estimated by men, but mothers consider them as safe partners for their daughters, and girls like them because they dance well, and don't bother them with conversation.

They appear to us to occupy the same relative position with regard to the *débutantes* of the season that professional jockeys bear to the favourites for the Derby and Oaks.

In fact, when a lady who breeds for the London market 'brings out' a daughter whom she considers likely to carry off one of the great stakes of the matrimonial lottery, she prefers entrusting her on grand occasions to the guidance of Alphonse Tiptoe rather than to that of any one who may hold an intermediate grade between that accomplished pupil of Madame Michau and the Marquis of Colchicum, the prize *parti* of the day.

In the first place Mrs. Rhino is aware that Alphonse knows if he were to presume to dream of making love to the innocent Eloise Rhino, she would treat him as unceremoniously as she would treat her butler under similar circumstances; and that all the capital dinners, and pleasant *soirées*, and morning polkeries in Grosvenor Square, and *déjeuners dinatoires* at Richmond, would, from that moment, belong rather to the Past than the Future.

Alphonse Tiptoe, therefore, thinks no more of committing such a folly than Jem Robinson does of buying the 'Merry Monarch' cheap to draw his one-horse chaise, but he waltzes smoothly, and gallops rapidly, and polks intricately, and shows his white teeth, and asks Eloise whether she was at the Opera on Tuesday, and whether she is going thither on Saturday: and enquires how she liked the last court-ball, and whether there was not a dreadful mixture at Mrs. Percy Smith's, and so on.

The Marquis of Colchicum, whose pensive air may be occasioned either by love, or by the wretched breed of foxes in the midland counties, looks coolly on, meanwhile, at Miss Rhino's many-twinkling feet, and sees her smiling and chattering earnestly with Alphonse, without feeling the smallest twinge of jealousy; for he is a man of the world, secure in his 20,000*l.* a year; he knows Alphonse's precise position in society—that he is poor, and a dancer by profession, and that the simple Eloise is too well-principled, and has been too carefully brought up, to think of anything but the pick of the peerage, for her first two seasons at least.

Mrs. Rhino contemplates the trio with materna

pride and anxiety, smiling approvingly at Alphonse's trained activity, and rivalling the electric telegraph by the delicacy and accuracy with which she works Eloise, who is as well broken in as an old pointer, and would no more think of listening to Alphonse when Lord Colchicum appeared disposed to talk to her, than the said pointer would deign to notice a lark, with a partridge under his nose.

In such little social scenes as these, Alphonse and his compeers play conspicuous parts, and so they lead pleasant, easy lives till their youth has glided away in one incessant twirl, and then, when baldness or grey hairs and corpulence assail them, and when their legs, their bread-winners, begin to fail, they shuffle off the stage of fashionable life, and nobody knows nor cares what becomes of them.

Some few, who have interest, settle down as Masters of the Ceremonies at Margate and Broadstairs, whilst others marry rich and hideous relicts of opulent tradesmen—but the demand for such desirable widow-women is said to be far greater than the supply.

Younger and more active members of the profession fill up their places at the dinner-tables and in the ball-rooms of London; their old partners, who are all married, and have houses in Belgrave Square, and from ten to fifteen children a-piece, hate them because they know too much about their ante-nuptial campaigns; dances from Australasia and the Polynesian Islands supersede the Polka and Cellarius of their youth; and the only consolation which remains to poor, fat, stupid, gouty old Jack Tiptoe (for his name wasn't Alphonse), whilst he leads the life of a cabbage in the corner of a second-rate club, is the retrospect of an actively spent life, which moralists assure us is a very agreeable thing to look back upon—and for Jack's sake we hope it is.

And yet in the face of all this an amateur asserts that Englishmen cannot waltz. Bah!

Cependant, il y a du bon dans son livre. He hints in conclusion at the disgraceful condition in which many very promising young ladies commence the London season.

No man in these enlightened days would be so foolish or so cruel as to attempt to distinguish himself in a quick thing from Milton Spinney on a horse fat and short of work. Yet how many girls do we see brought up to town in country condition, and expected, without any previous preparation, to go through the season with advantage to themselves and credit to their *chaperons*.

We again, in conclusion, entreat the amateur not to lay aside his pen until he has worked out the vein which he has so happily touched upon: he would confer a real blessing on mothers, far beyond the soothing syrup, if he would throw together a few chapters on the condition and training of young women for the London market, with instructions as to the quantity of walking exercises and alteratives requisite to enable them to polk till five in the morning without changing colour or turning a hair.

He cannot take a better model for his work than 'Nimrod on the Condition of Hunters.'

1845.

OUR CHAPEL OF EASE.

IT is a melancholy truth that, whilst most of the horrible cases of cruelty and oppression towards the slave population which formerly used to be sought out by the paid emissaries of the Emancipationists, and sent home, duly varnished and embellished, to harrow up the hearts of the mature virgins of Clapham and raise a roar of execration from amongst the ultra-philanthropists of Exeter Hall, might have been, and indeed were,[1] proved

---

[1] Mr. S—— sends home a startling account of a young niggerling having been made into pepperpot and devoured by some anthropophagous planters. The horrid statement is diffused rapidly over the United Kingdom by means of the public press; drawings appear in every shop window of a group of red-faced individuals, with Panama hats and pig whips, partaking of this novel black broth; meetings are convened; petitions are drawn up and signed by the very chimney-sweeps of Britain; old women curtail the number of lumps of sugar they were wont to take in their tea; horrified hack cabmen get drunk on gin and repudiate rum; Berbice coffee won't sell unless the grocers call it Mocha, and shop-keepers' wives prefer silk gowns to cotton ones on principle; in short, a

to be malicious falsehoods, or at most molehills magnified into mountains by venal ingenuity, nearly all that has been alleged respecting the moral darkness of our black brethren in bygone days, was founded on fact.

It is needless now to point out with whom the fault lay, the question is 'story done' as the niggers say; and if to promote the greatest happiness of the greatest number has been the desideratum of the present government, they may truly congratulate themselves on having attained their object. A few hundred white men and their families have certainly been reduced from opulence to penury, but, on the other hand, many thousand negroes have been placed in a position infinitely superior to that of the agricultural population of

severe blow is inflicted on the colonial character. Four months afterwards, it could not come sooner, a properly attested contradiction to Mr. S——'s story arrives through the governor of the colony. The pepperpot happened to be composed of a small black pig instead of a small black piccaninny. It is copied into one ministerial paper, the interest of the whole affair ceases. The provincial press don't care to circulate the disproval of the best tale of horror they have met with for years; and of the many thousand persons who read, believed, and shuddered at the story of colonial cannibalism, probably not a dozen ever hear that it was a lie.

any part of England. From the moment when a period was determined upon at which the slaves should become absolutely and unreservedly free, it became obviously as much the interest of the proprietors of estates to conciliate and improve the moral condition of their apprentices, as it ever could have been in slave time to overwork and retain them in ignorance.

Churches and schools were the first requisites which suggested themselves to such of the colonists as were enlightened enough to foresee that the sooner they could civilise and instruct the newly enfranchised negroes, the sooner they would be likely to induce them to listen to reason, return to their duty, and accept a fair remuneration for their labour.

Subscriptions were therefore set on foot in our parish for this laudable purpose. The parish church is seven miles from plantation Daageraad, on which I reside, and cannot contain one twentieth of the inhabitants of the parish. It was therefore proposed to erect a Chapel of Ease for the benefit of six or seven of those estates which were furthest from the existing church. The proprietor of

Daageraad contributed 100*l.*; the owners of the six adjoining plantations subscribed according to their means with equal liberality; the bishop of the diocese not only gave a large sum himself, but procured us 200*l.* from some benevolent society at home; and we at length found ourselves possessed of upwards of 1,300*l.* wherewith to defray the cost of erecting a building which should fulfil the double purpose of a place of worship and instruction.

A committee, composed of two or three planters of respectability and of an equal number of clergymen, was appointed to superintend the proper application of this money; and a long debate ensued as to the most eligible style of architecture to be adopted.

As all the buildings in Guiana are made of wood, there was no question as to the materials of which the new chapel should be composed.

The clerical part of the committee were desirous that it should be constructed and painted after the model of an English church, whilst the planters suggested, that as none of the negroes had ever seen one, and as they had consequently no prejudices to be shocked by the change, the building should rather resemble an Indian Logie or barn, open at the sides, and thatched thickly with troolie leaves at the top, a plan which would shelter the congregation better from the sun, admit more air, and accommodate four times the number of people, not to speak of the unsavoury odour of a close church with an overflowing negro congregation.

The clergymen—not seeing that this plan, which would have been a very indecent and improper one in Europe, had much in its favour on the coast of South America (where neither one style of building or another could possibly last twenty years on account of the dry rot and ants) —opposed it vehemently; and as they were gentlemen much beloved and respected by all classes the planters ultimately gave way to them, and a contract was entered into with a builder to construct a neat little white wooden church with a neat little white wooden steeple, and to roof it with shingles which were to be painted to look like slates.

When it was finished, painted, glazed, and

shingled, it looked very nice indeed, and very like one of those little churches one sees in boxes of Dutch toys; but in producing it the committee had unluckily expended all their money, and still there were neither seats nor pulpit nor fittings of any kind provided for the interior.

A bell,[1] too, as necessary an appendage to a church as a parson in the eyes of a negro, was wanting.

Whilst we were thus innocently and laudably employed in the pestilential[2] swamps of British Guiana, the before-mentioned ultra-philanthropists of Exeter Hall, and the elderly but energetic virgins of Clapham, seeing that period had been fixed upon for the emancipation of the slaves, and that the colonists were wisely endeavouring to meet the crisis in the best manner they could, began to feel that their occupation was going from them, and that their importance was somewhat

---

[1] I consider the negro bell-ringer as decidedly the happiest man I have ever yet seen, and the most important. He looks down on the parson immensely.

[2] All the island newspapers in speaking of Demerara invariably talk of our pestilential swamps with horror, lest their negroes should take it into their heads to come to a country where wages are treble what they are in Barbadoes, St. Lucia, &c.

lessened; they therefore determined upon having one more blow at us before they sank back into insignificance, and on endeavouring to see if they could not, by abridging the term originally agreed upon for the apprenticeship, and by letting the slave population loose on our hands before we were prepared for the measure, place us in what the Yankees term 'an unhandsome fix.'

They in consequence met, resolved, petitioned, published, agitated, mobbed the secretary for the colonies, flattered the under secretary, and bullied the government, until it was too happy to give us and our interests up to them in order to get rid of their anile importunities. The slaves were turned loose upon society before any laws were ready for their coercion; were very happy and very idle for a time, and now resist every necessary legislative enactment as an infringement of the absolute state of liberty, or rather anarchy, which they at first enjoyed. We—the whites—*are* in an unhandsome fix, and none of us know how we shall get out of it!

However, 'Nil desperandum' is our motto, and a very good one it is for people who have to struggle against such difficulties under such a sun. You hear people talk of living by the sweat of their brows in England; Lord help 'em! I should like to make them go to church here. They would see that we are obliged to save our souls as well as to maintain our bodies by the sweat of ours.

It had been at first the intention of the committee to have called upon the original subscribers for a further contribution towards the completion of our little chapel; but the total cessation of business, the sight of the canes rotting on the ground, and the enormous price demanded for labour, convinced the members of it that nothing more could reasonably be expected from that quarter.

So for five or six months nothing more was done. At last a good many of the free labourers returned to their duty; the planters, rather than see their estates relapse into swamps (which would very soon be the case if the drainage were not kept clear), decided on acceding to their extravagant demands; large sums were paid to them monthly as wages—far more than their necessities required —and the black population soon became possessed of more money than they well knew what to do with.

The clergyman of the parish, Mr. Croyle, a gentleman respected and beloved both by white man and negro, was of course anxious to see the new chapel in use, and perceiving that there was a good deal of money in circulation amongst the labourers, he proposed to endeavour to get them to contribute the sum requisite for its completion, about 300*l.*

He therefore wrote notes to the managers of the different estates, soliciting permission to come and make a collection for that purpose, and enquiring, shrewdly enough, on what day of the month it was customary to pay the people on each particular plantation.

He then preached a charity sermon on the subject, and obtained a very satisfactory collection amounting to nearly 50*l.* The days on which he intended to collect on the various estates were announced from the pulpit and published on the church door.

His success was great, and proved that if the negroes were eager to get money they were equally willing to part with it. I had no opportunity of attending any of his collections before he arrived at Daageraad on the evening of our pay day. He drove up the avenue in his gig just as we had finished our dinner.

We soon rigged him a sort of pulpit in the gallery before the house, where he established himself, having on the desk before him a ledger, pen and ink, two or three colonial Gazettes, and a large empty money-bag.

As pay-day is always a holiday, and as Mr. Croyle was expected, the people were all dressed in their best clothes and were sitting in groups under the palm trees of the avenue, full of fun, cracking their jokes on one another and upon us, and drinking bottled beer,[1] a very favourite beverage with them.

As soon as Mr. Croyle announced that he was ready, they all rose and crowded up into and under the gallery, the women, as usual, making most noise and giving most trouble.

He began by making them a speech, import-

---

[1] Small beer they term 'nigger beer,' bottled malt liquor 'gentleman porter.'

ing that their masters had very kindly built them a church when times were good and they had plenty of money; but that now they were no longer able to go to any further expense. That the negroes were themselves rich, and that he knew them well enough to know that they would be liberal in a matter like the present one, which concerned their own spiritual welfare and the education of their children, for the Chapel was to serve on week days as a school-house. He concluded by informing them that the name of every subscriber and the amount of his subscription should be printed in the 'Colonial Gazette.'

He next read to them the amount subscribed by the negroes on the estates where he had already collected, of course selecting the names of the most liberal contributors, just to give his audience an idea of what they ought to do.

He then addressed himself to the head cooper of Daageraad, an old African Mahometan, who, although converted, presented rather a singular admixture of Christianity and Mahometanism in his conversation and appearance. He was a very handsome old man with calm dignified manners and a long white beard; and as he stood by the side of Mr. Croyle, leaning on his staff, clothed in a flowing blue garment, he reminded me of the representations we see in old drawings of the saints and elders of the church.

Mr. Croyle addressed him thus:

'Demon, you are an excellent man; I have no parishioner who attends more regularly at church, or at the communion table, or who brings up his family more respectably; you shall head my list, I have no doubt but that you will contribute handsomely, for I know you can afford to do so.'

The venerable Demon answered this insidious appeal by a sort of oriental salaam, and remained silent.

'Well, my man,' pursued Mr. Croyle, 'what shall I put you down for?'

Demon fumbled in his pocket; hundreds of black eyes, and faces too, were watching intently his slightest movement. At last he enquired innocently:

'Massa, how much you charge?'

'Oh, my good fellow, I *charge* nothing; I

leave it entirely to your known piety and good feeling to set a good example to the gang.'

'Well, massa, s'pose me gib *one* dollar, dat good?

'Why, Demon, the head cooper at Mosquito Hall gave three dollars, and I should be sorry you gave less than him because he is not nearly so well-conducted a man as yourself; he drinks grog!'

'True massa? Mosquito Hall Jim gib tree dollar? Den me sall gib four; they nebber sall say dat dam grog-drinking nigger win o' Misser Robbins's head cooper!'

'Very well, my man; God bless you for your liberality. See here, I shall write down your name in this book, and have it printed in the 'Gazette."'

'Tankee, massa.'

'By the by, what *is* your surname?'

'Heigh, massa, me name Demon; manager nebber gib me oder name. Dat dam good un.'

'Well, but Demon, if I am to publish your name in the 'Gazette' I must publish your surname as well as your christian name.'

'Well, massa, me b'lang to Misser Robbins; he bery good massa; s'pose you write me Robbins too.'

As Demon Robbins therefore he was written down, and many of the people following his example I have no doubt but that some day the gazette in which the subscriptions of Daageraad are printed will be, at some Aldermanbury meeting, adduced as a conclusive proof of the loose lives and multitudinous bastards of the planters.

Demon Robbins, very well satisfied with himself, continued to stand by Mr. Croyle, acting the part of gentleman-usher to the people, who were rather slow in coming forward, though not from any unwillingness to contribute, as the result proved.

Romeo London, the captain of our schooner, a tall stout sulky-looking negro, next presented himself. He had listened attentively to what had passed between Demon and the parson, and slapped down at once four dollars, muttering as he walked off: 'Four dollar, too much money; nebber mind, when me for dead me shall go to heaven one time (at once).'

As London was a man of many wives, and an indifferent church goer, Mr. Croyle accepted his money without wasting his breath in eulogising his liberality.

A negro called Blake, a very fine young man of most industrious habits, now rushed up the steps, and having put down two dollars begged that the parson would intercede with me for him, as he wished to have a new house.

I told Mr. Croyle that his request was absurd, he occupied the very best house on the estate with his mother and young brother.

Upon this Blake stated that he had quarrelled with his mother and could live with her no longer. 'She too old and too cross!'

'But recollect, my good fellow, she is still your mother; she is old, and it is your duty to take care of her. You must not mind any little asperities of temper; you know that God Almighty commands you to honour your father and mother.'

'Iss, massa, me sabey dat dam well; but Goramity no sabey what my mother do to me last night. Me bring a gentleman eat foo-foo [1]

---

[1] Foo-Foo is the favourite and indispensable food of the negroes It is made of boiled plantains and salt fish pounded togetherwith a

wi' me, she no likee dat, so she kick de gentleman too bad behind, and box me all to pieces; and then she bite great bit out o' me, down here. Goramity no sabey dat!' quoth Blake, rubbing his posteriors.

Diana, the creole driver, or governess of black young ladies and gentlemen from the ages of ten to fifteen, followed. She paid a dollar for herself, another for her son, and offered a bit (4d.) for her daughter. Mr. Croyle said he was much obliged, but he could not receive such a small sum.

'Heigh, massa, dat plenty for me piccaninny, she bery small,' said Diana, evidently unconscious that a large soul might be packed in a small body.

Next came Yacky the blacksmith. He proposed giving a guilder (1s. 4d.), he vowed he could spare no more.

Mr. Croyle quietly observed that the Fearnought smith had subscribed very handsomely.

little water. A negro despises bread, biscuit, even fat pork, in comparison with a fresh plantain; and it is ludicrous enough to observe the importance which the nigger who is charged to compound foo-foo for a boat's crew assumes during the operation, which merely consists in mixing the two ingredients thoroughly with a little water.

Down came Yacky with three dollars instantly. 'Dey nebber sall say dat footy little coffee plantation win o' Misser Robbin's niggers.'

Mr. Croyle applauded the sentiment, bagged the money, and enquired if Yacky were regularly married to a very pretty girl with a child in her arms whom he had brought up to contribute her mite.

'No, massa, she no my wife in church yet; me got another lady in town, and two more piccaninny. When manager gib me new house den me sall hax you marry 'em both one time.'

As it was no time to discuss a point of negro morality, Mr. Croyle merely dismissed Yacky and his concubine with a frown, reserving what he had to say on the subject for a more convenient season.

Every negro on the plantation subscribed something; those who had no money to spare at the time promised certain subscriptions, which they all faithfully paid the next month, and the result of Mr. Croyle's activity was a sum of money sufficient to fit up the interior of the church very handsomely, and to build a large shed close by for the horses to remain under during service, for the head people on the estates generally are allowed to ride to church if there are any spare horses; it enhances their importance immensely in the eyes of the other 'dam low niggers' who have to walk.

April 22, 1847.

CHELSEA HOSPITAL

> Gravis annis
> Miles—multo jam fractus membra labore.
> HORAT. *Sat.* I. 1. 5.

I FEAR that it may appear presumptuous in an unknown writer to touch upon a subject which Mr. Gleig, that talented and estimable member of the Church Militant, has conducted through three octavo volumes;[1] yet I was so deeply moved by a visit which I made to Chelsea the other day that I cannot forbear committing to paper the details of one of the most agreeable mornings which it has ever been my good fortune to pass.

As a retreat for war-worn veterans who have done with the stirring scenes of life, and who only wish for an asylum whence they may sink down undisturbed into their graves at peace with God and man, I prefer the secluded locality of Chelsea to that of its more animated and noisy sister-

---

[1] *Chelsea Veterans*, by the Rev. G. R. Gleig, 1842, is probably the work alluded to.

establishment at Greenwich. Each is, however, admirably adapted to the description of persons which it contains. Seamen enjoy the seaport-like bustle of the river and its banks, whilst the habits of soldiers, who have been accustomed to live aloof in barracks, are more staid and regular; and, without intending any disrespect to the national ornament of the river Thames, or to the deserving old fellows whom it cherishes in its bosom, I fancy that the Pensioners at Chelsea are, owing to their limited numbers, a superior and better educated class of men than their brethren at Greenwich.

The Hospital is a plain old-fashioned building nearly concealed by enormous trees. No great thoroughfare approaches it, and I have little doubt but that many residents in London have never seen it. Few of the suburbs have undergone so little change as Chelsea; no railroad terminus, with its concomitant 'busses and cabs, steam engines and steam whistles, has as yet broken in on the repose of its old-fashioned inhabitants.

The botanical garden, celebrated for its cedars —now, alas! showing signs of decay—though obsolete, still exists; and excepting one gas manufactory I could not discover any new-fangled improvement of the nineteenth century likely to obtrude its officious advantages on the antiquated minds and habits of the neighbourhood.

At half past ten on Sunday morning I applied for admittance at the east gate of the Hospital, where sat a guard of old men clad in a costume which recalled to my mind Hogarth's picture of the 'March to Finchley.'

Being readily admitted I proceeded to the main quadrangle, where I found the Pensioners mustering for church parade. Men, maimed by every variety of mutilation under which life could be retained, were slowly gathering from the various wards.

Empty sleeves, wooden legs, bent backs, and disfigured features, bore witness that these gallant fellows had dearly bought, not the ease, for that few of them have health to know, but the repose which they enjoy.

Amidst all these signs of bodily weakness and infirmity I remarked an erectness of carriage and a neatness of dress which proved that neither age nor sickness could eradicate habits acquired by long service. You could read in every man's face that he respected himself and knew his own worth, and was proud that his country had recognised it.

The money expended on such an establishment as this is no charity, it is but the payment of a just debt. The Pensioners have no more than their deserts, and it is painful to think how many others there are who have equal claims on their country without the good fortune of having them thus acknowledged.

I could have mused over the interesting picture before me for hours, but the sound of drums and fifes broke in upon my reverie.

The old men formed in a double line on either side of the gravel walk, and the governor of the Hospital, preceded by a blind drummer and two octogenarian fifers, and accompanied by the officers of the establishment, appeared on the parade.

He is himself as shattered as the veterans over whose welfare he presides; an armless sleeve and an irregularity of gait declare that his have been no holiday campaigns.

One of his subs was minus a leg; and I was

informed that the other, a very fine-looking man, had received seven balls in various parts of his body.

The Pensioners were closely examined by their governor, as he limped along their most accurate line, with an air rather of affectionate interest than of official scrutiny.

Before they broke for chapel word was passed down their ranks that a pair of green spectacles had been picked up, and was in the hands of the adjutant. An ophthalmic Egyptian limped forth and claimed them, thus characteristically concluding this singular military spectacle.

The chapel is large and gloomy, but handsome. The altar is draped on either side with the banners of Hyder Ali and Tippoo Saib; over the heads of the congregation wave the standards of Napoleon's best troops, intermixed with tattered trophies from India and America; sixteen Imperial eagles adorn the walls, and attest the prowess of those soldiers of whom these veterans were once the flower.

The body of the church is entirely filled by the Pensioners; a single line of pews carried along the walls on either side accommodates the officers of the Hospital and their families.

It happened, at the time I visited the place, that these families contained several young women of great beauty, and never did female youth and loveliness stand forth more conspicuously than when contrasted with the Rembrandt-like heads and shattered frames of these venerable soldiers. Verily, it was a sight to make a man's heart leap in his bosom.

The service I thought well performed. The chaplain, Mr. Gleig, reads distinctly, but with a considerate rapidity, probably in order that his aged flock may not be fatigued by over much standing; there is but little singing, in which a few of the Pensioners and their children join; the organ is excellent.

I did not, however, so much admire Mr. Gleig's manner of reading the service as his demeanour in the pulpit.

His manly, straightforward, and kindhearted appeals to the common sense and professional character of his audience must strike every listener with respect and esteem.

His appointment did the highest honour to Lord John Russell, and forms one of the healthiest, though perhaps one of the humblest, leaves in the crown of laurel which that patriotic statesman has so diligently earned and so richly deserved.

The poor old Pensioners were pleased at the notice of the Minister, and felt grateful that he had appointed as their chaplain one of themselves, as it were, who could understand their feelings and sympathise with their infirmities.

What shall I say of the congregation, having thus eulogised the clergyman?

In most assemblies of men, we know to our cost if we have lived long enough, that the majority are but of average merit, that many sink below mediocrity, and that few rise above it.

But here, amidst this strange collection of cripples, all have been actually tried in the fire and not found wanting; all have approved themselves brave, obedient, and faithful; have undergone severe and bloody trials in every quarter of the globe, wherever their duty led them, and have been fortunate to have their merits recognised and their toils rewarded by the 'otium cum dignitate' of Greenwich.

Hackneyed as that phrase is, I know of none other which so well expresses the position of these meritorious servants of England.

Immediately after church, dinner is served out in the hall, which is likewise shaded by banners pierced and rent by shot, and bearing the words Jena, Friedland, Austerlitz, &c.

The Pensioners carry their food off to their wards, where they dine in messes arranged by themselves. The cooking is savoury and good. They receive no spirits, but each man is allowed a pint and a half of porter daily.

They are very courteous to strangers, whom they generally invite into their wards, which are beautifully clean, and are furnished with every comfort calculated to promote their ease and well-being. There is a good library open for their use, as well as a large and warm smoking-room when the weather is cold.

I was about to leave the Hospital, well satisfied with my visit, which I promised myself to repeat at the first opportunity, when a tall old Pensioner touched his hat to me and accosted me by name. I recognised him as having filled the office of porter for many years at a house where I was in the habit of visiting.

On expressing my surprise at seeing him at Chelsea, he informed me that he had served for twenty years in the Life Guards, and had been wounded at Waterloo. When he found the work of his situation becoming too hard for his old age, he applied to his former colonel, now General L——, who readily procured him admission into the Hospital.

He spoke highly of his present position, saying that the greatest grumbler could find no fault with it. He added: 'We used to find our time hang heavy on our hands, Sir, having nothing to do, until Lord John gave us our little gardens; since then we have had something to take an interest in.'

Mr. Gleig, in his work on Chelsea, mentions that Lord John Russell had caused a sort of common field adjoining the Hospital to be enclosed and divided into small squares containing a rood each, and had furnished the Pensioners with tools and seeds for its cultivation.

I accompanied the ex-Life Guardsman in order to judge of the success of his sword when modified into a hoe, and beheld one of the prettiest specimens of humble gardening that can be imagined.

On an eminence overlooking the field, a rustic summer-house had been erected, where four or five veterans sat smoking their pipes; whilst the red coats of others were visible dotted about the green garden (which contains three or four magnificent trees), picking flowers for their visitors or contemplating their tiny crops with a grave interest rendered almost ludicrous by the limited extent of their culture.

My friend had planted about a square yard of carrots, which had failed; but he had the primest bed of onions in the whole field, and at each corner of his demesne swaggered a tall hollyhock, on which he seemed to pride himself hugely. He informed me that he purposed replacing the carrots by eight cabbages, from which he anticipated great things, and said that his plantation of musk, which he retailed in penny pots to the children of the neighbourhood, was as good as sixpence a week to him.

I could not help muttering to myself Juvenal's

> Est aliquid quocunque loco quocunque recessu,
> Unius dominum sese fecisse lacertæ.

Having spent some time loitering about these interesting specimens of military gardening, the old man told me that he was going to see his grandson, who had lately been elevated to the post of triangler in the band of the Duke of York's school.

We therefore walked together up to that noble institution just as the gates were opened and the boys paraded in front of the building. They were clean smart lads from six to fourteen years of age, and to my unprofessional eyes appeared to manœuvre excellently well considering their various ages and stature.

The band played several marches and overtures with great precision, although they certainly did not average eleven years all round.

My old Pensioner's grandson afforded him infinite delight. The little fellow was just seven years old, and was mightily puzzled to keep step with his comrades as they marched and countermarched, playing all the time.

At three o'clock they went off to their church, and I returned to the Hospital to listen to another of Mr. Gleig's excellent discourses.

THE END.

www.ingramcontent.com/pod-product-compliance
Lightning Source LLC
Chambersburg PA
CBHW030752230426
43667CB00007B/933